Power to Manage Yourself

Power to Manage

Yourself

~~~~~~~~~~~~~~~~~~~~~~~~~~~~~~~~~~~~~~

by

HAROLD BLAKE WALKER

H|B

Harper & Brothers Publishers, New York

Library of Congress catalog card number: 55-8529

To the memory of
My Father

CONCORDIA
COLLEGE AND
HIGH SCHOOL

Gift of
Pastor Braunschweiger

Contents

Foreword

The insecurity and the tempo of our times have placed constantly increasing strains on human personality. Those of us who counsel with men and women are disturbed by the fact that so many people are coming apart at the seams, going to pieces under the stress of harsh experience. Guilt and frustration, fear and the feeling of futility beat against the ramparts of the self, and men are overwhelmed.

We wonder anxiously if a man can be the master of his fate. Is it possible to take life in our hands and fashion it for triumph despite the pressures that bear upon us? Can we manage ourselves, even when circumstances seem to be the arbiter of our fate? Above all, is there any real meaning in the struggle of life that makes the fight to live worth the effort?

We are somewhat like a small boy tugging at his father's coattails, pointing to the telegram in his father's hands, and asking: "What does it say? What does it say?" So, you and I pull at the coattails of our experience, asking: "What does it say?" We blunder into frustration and failure, fear and insecurity and we wonder what they have to say to us. Is there any meaning in our struggle for existence? Is life worth what it costs when we meet obstacles on every road we travel and when "fears assail and doubts annoy"? In plain language, "What does life say?"

There are those to whom life seems to say nothing at all. It is only a meaningless round of getting through one week after another, haunted by frayed nerves and impossible tensions. There are those who have been liberated from the faith of the ages and with the help of a psychoanalyst are enduring their liberty unhappily. There are those who are world weary and exhausted by the trivialities on which they waste their days. Life, for them, has nothing important to say, so there is no point to listening. Maybe they turn into cynics, or tired idealists with a chip on their shoulders and a sneer for life.

On the other hand, there are men and women who listen for the wisdom of life and look beyond the isolated moment in time toward the long reach of tomorrow. They know instinctively that life has something to say if they can learn to read its mystery. They are inwardly certain that life does not walk on aimless feet, and they want to know what stumbling blocks mean and whether steep, rocky trails have significance they can find. Can they make anything worth while out of their frustrations or fashion their souls on the insecurity in which they live?

This book is intended for those who wish to grow by way of their problems and hurts and to find some reason for conquering their own weaknesses and inadequacies. It is for those who wish to discover the resources of God with which they may be enabled to manage their own lives creatively.

I am grateful to my secretary, Mrs. Audrey Morrison, for her unusual care in preparation of the manuscript, to the loyal and helpful congregation of the First Presbyterian Church, to Mrs. Margueritte Harmon Bro for her critical reading of the manuscript in its preliminary form, to John Stettner, my colleague, for his suggestions, and to my wife, whose discerning suggestions and constant search for material were a vital resource. To my wife and three sons, Herbert, Howard, and Timothy, I am grateful for their patience and understanding.

HAROLD BLAKE WALKER

First Presbyterian Church
Evanston, Illinois

Power to Manage
Yourself

CHAPTER I

Your Responsibility for You

A SUCCESSFUL and yet inwardly troubled man opened a conversation in my study with the question, "Why is it that I can manage my business so well and at the same time I cannot manage my own life?" The answer is, of course, that it is infinitely easier to manage a business, a club, or a church than it is to manage yourself. Alexander the Great was master of all he surveyed. He ruled the world, but he never succeeded in mastering himself. He conquered everything except himself, and died in a drunken brawl.

Even a little honest introspection makes it plain that you are your own most difficult problem. You have yourself on your hands morning, noon, and night. You can run away from your business, but you cannot run away from yourself. Sooner or later you are constrained to take yourself in hand in the sure knowledge that if you do not, life will turn into the dust and ashes of failure and regret. And yet, in the hour that you resolve to manage yourself creatively you come face to face with the stern fact of your spiritual need. Your apparent resources seem altogether inadequate to undergird your responsibility for you.

The businessman who lamented his inability to manage himself confessed readily that in his business he hired the best accountants he could find, the best production manager, and the best sales manager. He employed a top-notch tax expert to figure his taxes. He got the best possible advice from efficiency experts and laboratory research. He had studied his business until he knew it fore and aft and in between. Actually, he left no stones unturned in order to assure the wise management of his business.

Unhappily, his own life was a different matter. There was nothing efficient about it. The management was far below par. He admitted he was becoming an alcoholic. He was having trouble with his wife and he did not know how to deal with his children. He was tense and irritable and miserably unhappy. What on earth was wrong? He said quite frankly that he never before had consulted anyone he could call an expert on living abundantly. He had read no books designed to help men like himself. He had barely a speaking acquaintance with the Bible and he confessed he did not know how to pray.

Of course, if he had sought guidance and help for his own life as zealously as he had sought wisdom in the operation of his business, the executive would not have blundered into his tangled situation. Fortunately, he was wise enough to recognize that he was so muddled he needed outside help to unravel his problem. What the troubled man needed was somebody who would be the spiritual equivalent of an efficiency expert. His condition required someone who could help him to see himself and his human relations with some objectivity.

Before he could take command of his situation it was necessary for him to see that he was suffering, for one thing, from a dated emotion, a hangover from his childhood. In his home his mother had been the general manager in a large way, ruling everybody in the household by hook or by crook. He did not know it, but his hostility to his mother had turned into a powerful determination to be the master of his own household. He could not untangle the problems of his upset home until he became aware that his tyranny at home was not the virtue he thought, but was rather a psychological throwback to his own childhood experience.

Then, too, having achieved considerable success, he had arrived at the top of the hill. Everything seemed to have been accomplished. He had gotten what he wanted, reached the goals he had set, and life had lost its meaning. Now there was nothing to challenge his faith or his courage as there had been during the years of struggle and hardship on the road up. Travel and golf and fishing were pleasant enough as diversions, but they did nothing to renew his sense of direction or purpose. They offered no essential meaning for his life. He needed to see that alcoholism was his means of escape from boredom, from life without a core of vital meaning. In order to recover it was imperative that he discover a sense of spiritual mission and moral direction.

Finally, it was apparent that success in business had led the man in question to assume that his failure at home was not his fault. It seemed to him reasonable to believe that if he got along well at the office, made money, and was respected in the business community, the trouble at home was the fault of the family. Success in one area should automatically guarantee success in the other if the people in one place were reasonable like the people in the other. So he blamed his wife and children for his tension, his alcoholism, his conflicts. It was imperative for him to recognize that his tyranny, his selfishness, and his confidence that he knew better than anyone else in the family were the sources of his trouble.

After some months of counseling, talking it out, learning to recognize his dated emotion, to understand the need for spiritual meaning, and to discover the significance of fellowship and co-operation at home, the business executive began to achieve a better adjustment to life. Through spiritual exercises he found new poise and powers to manage himself and he began to see himself and his human relationships in clearer perspective. Unfortunately, he had wasted long years in unnecessary misery and conflict. He might very well have studied his life as he studied his business and sought and found the resources for successful living as he sought and found the resources for a successful business career.

Many of us are like that business executive. We know our lives are at sixes and sevens and we are not managing our lives either efficiently or creatively. We are not quite sure where we went off the track or why. Sometimes, like a young lady I know, we get to the point of thinking the world is all wrong and there is no hope of joy and not much point to going on. We want things to be right, but they seem to go wrong in spite of us. Upset and in conflict with ourselves we are like accidents going somewhere to happen. We seem to attract trouble like a magnet. We never seem to do or say the right thing at the right time.

The crux of the matter is the question: Are we able to manage ourselves? Can we take the stuff of which we are made and fashion it for triumph? Can we take our minds and our emotions and our wills and manage them with the wisdom of God? Or are we bound to run off the road into the morass of misery and conflict? There are times when we wonder. Wistfully and sadly we say when life slips out of control, "I wasn't myself when I did that," and it is true enough. With a bit of an ache in the heart we say, "I didn't mean to," as if our behavior ran off and left our intentions behind. Exasperated, we ask ourselves, "Now why did I do that?" as if some imp of perversity pushed us to folly when we were looking in the opposite direction.

The question of a small boy after he had been vigorously spanked is suggestive. "Mom," he asked tearfully, "how do you make yourself do what you ought to do?" That is the ultimate question, and often we hate ourselves because we do not know the answer. Our experience leads us to a fundamental contradiction. On one hand, we are confronted by the obvious fact that we are responsible for ourselves, and on the other hand, we face the realization that our lives have become unmanageable.

If we would discover how to do what we ought to do, we had best begin with the questions: Why are we victims rather than self-managers? Why do we go off the track and turn life into a long-term migraine headache? Psychologists and theologians have been wrestling with these questions for some time past. Psychologists insist that our lack of self-direction is evidence of immaturity, while theologians tell us we are victims of "original sin." Actually the psychologists and the theologians are not too far apart in their diagnosis. Immaturity is essentially failure to outgrow our "egocentric" predicament. "Original sin" is the "egocentric predicament," the self-centered, self-pleasing disposition that has to be overcome on the road to maturity.

There is more than a hint of our human predicament in the cartoon strip "Dennis the Menace." It began in a very human way when Hank Ketchum came home from work one evening and found his wife suffering the exasperation only a mother can know. "Hank," she said to her husband, "our son Dennis is a menace."[1] That started it. Hank, a cartoonist, knew a good title when he heard it. So Dennis goes his uninhibited way in cartoons full of insight into the life of a boy. He is a menace, like most of our children. Sometimes I wonder if he ever will grow from menace to manhood, from immaturity to maturity.

The trouble with Dennis is that he is a victim of the "egocentric," "self-regarding," or "self-pleasing" disposition. That is to say, he wants to do and to have what pleases him. Even by the time he is five or six years old he has very little notion of obligations or responsibilities. He is annoyed by duties. They interfere with what he thinks pleases him. His whole life is organized, or disorganized, around his ego. He pulls the cat's tail because it pleases him, and he has no notion of the cat's rights. He teases his little brother because it pleases him to annoy one who has usurped a portion of his mother's affection. He has no idea of sharing anything if he can help it. He smashes his toys because he feels like it, for he has not arrived at any appreciation of value.

Normally we expect Dennis to mature, to discover that there are some things in life more important than pleasing himself. Unfortunately Dennis sometimes matures chronologically without maturing psychologically or spiritually. He has a fringe of gray hair, but essentially he remains "Dennis the Menace," still pushing through life intent upon pleasing himself. He is miserably unhappy, confused and burdened by inner conflict. He is the gangster, intent upon doing what pleases him, regardless of the welfare of society. He is the practical joker, enjoying the discomfort of his victims. He is the adolescent girl, poorly adjusted to her own generation and at odds with her parents. He is the corrupt politician, wanting what pleases him at the expense of the public.

Van Wyck Brooks notes that Jack London destroyed himself because he never outgrew his ego, and in the end his "thirst for money and power destroyed the artist in him." He liked to be called "Mr. God" by his Korean valet in the days when he was the most highly paid writer in the world. Jack London was "Dennis the Menace" with little but years added to his stature. He did not understand his frustrations or comprehend the reason for the dust and ashes he felt in his soul. Why he was unpopular as a man was beyond his comprehension.

It should be noted that all of us are "Dennis the Menace" to ourselves and to society until we get ourselves out of our own way and discover something more important to be the focal center of meaning for our lives. Unhappily, however, the "self-pleasing" disposition in all of us is deeply rooted. It is the essence of what ancient theologians called our "depravity." Whatever we call it, it does not please us to face the fact that our self-pleasing disposition is the root of most of our ills.

Like the business executive, we block our own recovery by finding scapegoats outside of ourselves. It pleases us to save face; it displeases us to confess our own personal failure to meet life creatively. So we defend ourselves and make excuses in order to preserve the ego intact. We are pleased to claim credit for our virtues and our achievements; but we are equally displeased to accept responsibility for our failures and mistakes. It pleases us to have our pie and eat it too! So our sins are not our fault; another is to blame. Our problems are not of our own making; they are the result of forces beyond our control. We please ourselves and preserve our self-regard by getting out from under responsibility for being the way we are.

The ancient story of Adam and Eve is as modern as your morning newspaper. Adam, so the account runs, ate fruit picked from the forbidden tree because it pleased him, but he promptly felt guilty. He excused himself by insisting Eve was to blame. As he explained to the Lord, "The woman whom thou gavest me . . . she gave me fruit of the tree and I ate."[2] The poor man must have been something of a mouse, an ancient version of Mr. Milquetoast! Eve was the villain of the cast; or was she? She did not wish to be the villain and besides, she had a glib tongue and a quick wit. "The serpent beguiled me," she explained, pointing to the defenseless reptile, who could not talk back. The poor fellow did not have a chance. Condemned without a hearing, he and his offspring have been unpopular ever since.

Adam and Eve set the pattern for human behavior and the

pattern has not changed much since their day in the Garden of Eden. We get ourselves into fixes of one sort or another trying to please ourselves and then we look around for somebody to blame for our troubles. If we cannot find a convenient villain we imagine one. The villain, of course, robs our problems of their meaning and leaves us as we were. Listening day by day to the troubles of people I am amazed by the ingenious alibis they invent to escape responsibility for their own weaknesses. When things go wrong in their homes men offer a modern version of Adam's complaint: "The woman thou gavest me" is driving me to distraction. Neurotic women insist, "The children thou gavest me" are ungrateful. "They are making me miserable." The ineffective workman explains his failure by complaining, "The foreman had it in for me." The lazy student says he "flunked" because "My chemistry teacher did not like me." The spoiled child explains the fact that the neighborhood children pick on him by claiming they are "roughnecks." A poorly adjusted woman blames her unhappiness on the fact that "My mother never really loved me," as if that ended the matter.

The assumption behind the excuses we make for ourselves is that if we can discover alibis outside of ourselves we can escape responsibility for being the way we are. It is not our fault. Abraham Lincoln put it aptly when he explained the character of a village scoundrel by saying: "He's got the can't-help-its." The man was forever explaining his behavior in terms of people and things over which he had no control. Other people made him the way he was and he could not help it. The world is full of people who have "the can't-help-its." Shakespeare's word is appropriate, for we often talk as if we were "villains by necessity; fools by heavenly compulsion."[3] So we learn nothing from our folly and find no means for growth in hurts we bring upon ourselves.

There are three basic fallacies in our thinking that make it relatively easy for us to escape responsibility for ourselves. There is, of course, the popular notion that "you can't change human nature." When you reduce that idea to its personal equation, the essence of it is: "I cannot change me." Therefore, Q.E.D., I can't help being the way I am! I was born that way. So, if we are neurotic, strained by tension, frustrated, dishonest, failures, or anything else, we are simply a facsimile of plain human nature and we can't help it. We provide ourselves with a bullet-proof excuse for staying precisely as we are. What is more, we rob life of the meaning that comes from self-conquest.

But human nature can and does change. People do learn to manage themselves. One tense, "self-pleasing," ruthless man I knew had a heart attack, and in the face of it he had two choices. He could go on being the way he was and be the central figure for a fine funeral. He could change and live. His friends said he could not change and gave him six months to live. But he did change. In quietness and prayer he changed his pace and he changed his spirit, until he is one of the most poised and gentle men I know. He still runs his business effectively, but he is a different man. Employees who despised him now love him; those who once feared him have an affection for "the old man." He has gone on now ten years since his heart attack, a living illustration of the fact that God can change human nature.

Or there is the businessman who came to himself a few years ago after his wife died. Through the years he had played golf on Sunday mornings, thought religion was designed for the weak, mostly for women, and generally ran in hard and fast company. Material values were final for him and if principle got in the way of profit, so much the worse for principle. The death of his wife made him acutely aware of what he had missed and of his own need for something more dependable than his stocks and bonds. Quite literally he turned over a new leaf and set out to write a new chapter of his life. He resigned as a director of one company because he could not go along with unethical methods of doing business and he could not persuade his fellow directors to change their ways. He became an avid reader of the Bible and thoroughly honest in his pursuit of spiritual values at the expense of material values. He tells me quite frankly that he spent the first half of his life living by the assumption "You can't change human nature," and the first half of his life he views as a failure, even though he was decidedly a financial success. He has been living the second half of his life on the faith that "God can change human nature," and the second half promises infinitely more than the first.

The second fallacy in our contemporary thinking is simply a refinement of the first. It is the curious but common notion that, human nature being what it is, it is unfair to put character under strain. Editorial comment at the time of the West Point cribbing scandal noted that "putting a man on his honor not to cheat subjects him to terrific strain." Therefore, "monitoring students during examinations is a better system." West Point officials were condemned roundly because they trusted in "the honor of the corps" and made it relatively easy for men to cheat. Editorial writers seemed to be saying: It is all very well to have an honor system, but you had better relieve students of the unnecessary strain involved in being honest. You really cannot expect a man to be responsibile for integrity if you tempt him.

Basically, all this is like saying: You must not put Abraham Lincoln under stress and make him choose between deception and forthrightness in an election campaign. He might crack under the strain. Actually it is plain as a pikestaff that the character of Lincoln was nourished and strengthened on moral struggle. Indeed, the meaning of strain became clear in the character that emerged from it. Integrity that never has been subjected to strain is only a poor facsimile of the real thing; and honor that has not gone through the fires of temptation is only a mirage. Character is tempered and fused by the stresses it meets on Main Street. You cannot monitor the honesty of the neighborhood grocer or the man who runs the corner drugstore. He has to monitor himself through strain, temptation, and testing. He is responsible for his own integrity, and strain is part of the price he pays for honor.

What is more, it is clear that what someone has called "the moral grandeur of independent integrity" is established under stress. To be sure, one basketball star is corrupted by the offer of a bribe to throw a game; but another grows in stature by blunt refusal. One government official is destroyed by the lure of easy money; the other achieves moral greatness. When the crowd is bent on folly, having lost its head, one man goes along like a good fellow; but another grows in moral dignity standing alone. Strain builds one and destroys the other. Personality necessarily and inevitably is subjected to moral stress, but the outcome depends on something in the man.

The third fallacy in our thinking which enables us to run out on our responsibility for ourselves is the idea that character is merely the product of social environment. We simply "Do as the Romans do" because it comes naturally and we cannot be expected to do anything else. We all have to be like two peas in a pod! That, of course, lays a foundation for the notion that if you go wrong doing what everybody else is doing it is your neighbor's fault. The report of the Congressional Committee on Ethical Standards in Government reflects the idea that corrupt government officials are not really to blame. On the contrary, they are simply public illustrations of private moral standards from New York to Los Angeles.

No doubt it is true that individuals do reflect the behavior patterns of their communities, but that is no reason to conclude that an individual cannot be better than his society. There is no justification for the assumption that we cannot expect individuals to be better than their communities. Indeed, the whole philoso-

phy of the Christian faith rests on the conviction that men can
be better than their times, and progress is possible simply because
better men can make better communities. The prophets of Israel,
towering above their contemporaries in public thinking and
private living, are the glory of Israel. Socrates, standing alone
for something better than the Greeks of his time, gave dignity
to the Golden Age of Pericles. The simple truth is that we can
be better than our environment and nobler than our society.

Commonly the fallacy of blaming our failures and our personal difficulties on our social environment provides what might
be called a circumstantial alibi. We escape responsibility for our
behavior or our psychological condition by telling ourselves we
are victims of circumstances. We excuse ourselves by saying we
were "fenced in" and we did the only thing we could "under
the circumstances." You fight with your wife and you tell yourself, "Under the circumstances, how could I help it?" You resort
to unethical behavior in business and then salve your conscience
by telling yourself: "Under the circumstances, I could not do
anything else." As a politician, you find yourself under pressure
to approve a policy you believe to be wrong, but you say:
"Under the circumstances, I had to vote for it." You feel guilty
about the things you do, you even hate yourself, but you try to
escape from responsibility by pleading extenuating circumstances. It pleases you to escape responsibility.

Joseph Wood Krutch notes wisely that nine-tenths of the
people of the world think they are what they are and do what
they do because of circumstances and social pressures. He
observes that Henry Thoreau, discouraged, frustrated, and dis-
satisfied with himself, went away to Walden Pond and found
himself with two basic questions that concern you as much as
they concerned him. He asked himself: Am I the way I am
because of circumstances? Or are circumstances my master
because of me? These two questions are by no means academic;

your destiny depends upon the answer you give. If you rest your life on the alibi that you are what you are because of circumstances, you will excuse yourself for everything and stay the way you are. On the other hand, if you conclude you have become the victim of circumstances because of some inadequacy in yourself, then you are faced with the disturbing idea that you had better take command of yourself.

Obviously, you cannot escape from the circumstances that circumscribe your life. You were born into the world of the twentieth century, with all of its tensions and strains. You were reared in a particular family in a place you did not choose. You went to a neighborhood school and met children who happened also to live in the same neighborhood. You got a job that happened to be available in a place that was accessible. You endured sickness, disappointment, and frustration not of your own choosing. You met innumerable circumstances that conspired against the achievement of either character or success. You lived in a setting that in many ways determined the way of your going. It is trite, therefore, to say you cannot escape circumstances.

It is important to notice, however, that circumstances are by no means the final arbiter of your destiny. In the final summing up, what your environment does to you depends upon what it finds in you. The "sidewalks of New York" beget both character and corruption. The small town, with all its limitations, rears both little men with little minds and big men with big minds. Lack of opportunity or privilege has a hand in creating both the weak and the strong and wealth and social place have a hand in making both the useless and the useful. There is something in you that determines what conditions do to you.

It may please you to escape your responsibility for you by one device or another, but the first step toward responsible self-management is honest recognition of your responsibility for you.

Face yourself bluntly and stop making excuses. Alibis are a luxury you cannot afford because they thwart your discovery of the basic illness in you. Honest self-examination is the beginning of your maturity. Growth becomes possible only when you take a sober look at the menace in yourself and confess that it is there. Certainly the growth of the disciples began with the question, "Master, is it I?" We call the disciples saints now, but the night they sat together at the Last Supper they were not saints by any possible stretch of the imagination. They had quarreled over the chief seats in the Kingdom of God. They had wanted to destroy an unfriendly Samaritan village. Shortly, they were to desert their Master. One of them would betray him, another deny him, and in the stress of the Garden of Gethsemane "they all forsook him and fled."[4]

Nevertheless, Jesus believed in the twelve. Quite possibly he trusted in the mood in them which revealed itself at the Last Supper when he calmly announced: "One of you will betray me."[5] He noted that not one of the twelve looked at another of the company to ask, "Is it he?" On the contrary, there was a searching of souls and a single question from the lips of each of those who sat with Jesus: "Master, is it I?" The sainthood of the twelve began with that question, for it reflected an honest awareness of the menace in each one. They still were self-possessed and still would seek to save themselves when crisis came. They knew in their own minds that any one of them was capable of betrayal.

We do nothing to change ourselves until we know we are a menace as we are. We start to "climb the steep ascent of heaven" and to hear what life has to say only when we are aware we have made the hell we know. There is promise and there is hope when we begin to ask, "Master, is it I?" when life has lost its luster and we are plagued by tensions and fears, frustrations and conflicts. At the least we know where to begin, and sense that even if we were to change the outward scenery of our lives the pattern of the play would be the same without a change of inner character.

The second step toward responsible self-management involves a conscious shifting of our deepest concern from the "ego" to the "alter," from self to others. Our sustaining satisfactions come from contribution to the common life we share. Life finds fulfillment, not in getting, but in giving; not in saving altogether for ourselves, but in spending for the common good. A small girl felt the truth after a round of neighborhood visits, during which she acquired cookies, candy, and a collection of trinkets. When her mother reproved the little lady for bothering the neighbors and for an over indulgence of the acquisitive instinct, the child replied: "Oh the neighbors wanted me to come. I'm somebody they can give things to."

Quite possibly the need to give both ourselves and things to others is our response to what we feel of debt to those whose lives sustain us. As Paul noted, "I am under obligation both to the Greeks and to the barbarians; both to the wise and to the foolish."[6] We are debtors to philosophers and teachers, friends and loved ones whose wisdom has made us wiser than we might have been. The living and the dead have conspired to surround us with knowledge for "the kingdom of the mind." Faith and courage often are the gifts of those with whom we have traveled through some "valley of the shadow." Their wisdom lingers in the insights we have won. Their faith endures like anchors to windward when storms blow in from the deep. Their courage lies beneath our surface and seeming as the often undiscovered "hero of the soul." To be sure, we take the raw materials of our comradeships and human contacts, our rubbing elbows with the wisdom of the ages, and fashion them into ourselves, and yet we are debtors to all who have touched our lives in one way or another.

We are debtors, and in unconscious depths a sense of obligation lingers. So life goes wrong and inner conflicts rage when the menace of the "ego" obscures the rightful claim of the "alter." Frustration, futility, and inner conflict claim us when in nothing more than "getting and spending" we "lay waste our days." Tension crowds our tortured lives when grasping days follow one another in plodding procession. But looking outward with compassion and concern for the needs and hopes of other travelers on the road of life relieves the pent-up strain of serving nothing larger than "the little aims that end with self."

Deficit financing either in dollars or in the affairs of the spirit breeds anxiety and insecurity. A sense of shame that often hides beneath the surface of the soul plays havoc with the peace of mind that even selfish people seek. I learned the sobering truth long years ago by way of a boyhood charge account inspired by my fondness for a drugstore concoction called a "Grizzly Bear." It was made of two dippers of chocolate ice cream, chocolate and marshmallow syrup, nuts, and a red cherry to top it all. Unfortunately, I seldom had the fifteen cents necessary to acquire my favorite dish.

One day as I sat disconsolately beside a friend who was enjoying the delights of a Grizzly Bear, he suggested it was simple enough to open a charge account with the kindly proprietor of the drugstore. The idea seemed attractive, so I opened an account and had a Grizzly Bear. Thereafter, I indulged frequently in my favorite concoction. But on the first of the month I was considerably upset when I received a bill for two dollars and ten cents. My bank account would not cover such a contingency. It seemed unwise to inform my father of my charge account.

The more I wrestled with my problem, the worse I felt. I was ashamed and fearful and vastly troubled. My first reaction was to avoid the drugstore. I would walk around the block to escape the necessity of passing Mr. Sotgie's Pharmacy. Nevertheless, an inner demon pursued me. There seemed but one way out. I plagued the neighbors for odd jobs until I managed to gather two dollars and ten cents. It was a thrilling day of freedom and release when I finally paid the bill I owed and satisfied the debt that had weighed me down and troubled my days and my nights.

The truth, I think, is clear. We cannot run a charge account against the world, claiming what we want for ourselves and giving nothing in return. Somehow the soul rebels against the huge, relentless army of the world's desires that turns life in upon itself and leaves a legacy of inner turmoil. Life seems like one blunder after another rather than an orderly progression until we shift the emphasis from "ego" to "alter," from self to others. But when life ceases to be preoccupied with getting and becomes concerned with giving, closed doors begin to open and life assumes a new dimension of manageable strength and freedom.

The third step toward responsible self-management is faith to believe that there are saving spiritual possibilities in every situation. When we shift the focus of our lives from self to others to satisfy the social debt we feel, we meet the mystery of a new and saving dimension in our lives. Theologians would call it "the grace of God." The word "grace" is important. It suggests something done for us that we cannot do for ourselves, as if under certain conditions there occurs "a gentle conspiracy of nature" and of God that lifts us out of darkness into light. Jesus put the matter simply when he said: "Where two or three are gathered in my name, there am I in the midst of them,"[7] healing, lifting, guiding, and inspiring.

It is curious how human conflicts growing from the menace in ourselves are often healed beyond our conscious will, as when a man I know whose life was threatened by the hatred of another found that hatred turning into friendship when he joined his enemy in a common struggle to overcome a dread disease. "Where two or three are gathered" serving worthy goals beyond themselves, the Holy Spirit adds a saving, healing power, lifting each above himself, out of "ego," into God. When we dare to lose ourselves, lose sight of ourselves, in devotion to some worthy end, there is a conspiracy of grace that lifts us out of conflict and frustration, into freedom and "the peace that passeth all understanding."

It seems strange at times how half-forgotten memories come back to light the road ahead with wisdom quite unheeded in the past. One such memory pushed its way into my mind, reminding me of a boyhood foursome we were wont to call "The Four Horsemen." We worked and played together, fought together, and got into trouble together. On one occasion we were close to blows. Harsh words had been uttered and threats voiced while we were on our way home from school after an annoying brush with education through the day. We were on the brink of a real battle when we were hailed by an old gentleman sitting at the wheel of a two-cylinder Maxwell automobile. He said his auto simply would not run and would we push him to the combination livery stable and garage three blocks away?

We put our shoulders to the car and slowly moved it foot by foot. We huffed and puffed and slapped each other on the back. Laughter punctuated our pushing, and in due time we reached the garage where the combination blacksmith-mechanic helped us push the offensive automobile inside. The job was done! Our quarrel was done, too, and "The Four Horsemen" were one again. Our differences, born in "ego" had been dissolved in our devotion to a common task to which we gave our strength. We lost sight of ourselves pushing. It was as if where four were gathered in a kindly service. Another was at work healing a conflict four alone could never heal.

So in every situation where the menace of unfettered ego has brought life to frustration or conflict there is a saving spiritual possibility when we lose sight of ourselves in devotion to some worthy end beyond ourselves. There is a power beyond us waiting for a chance to heal and lift. As Jesus noted, "Behold, I stand at the door and knock," but the key is inside, in the willingness to lose the ego, whose unneighborly self-seeking keeps the door to spiritual power both locked and bolted.

There is, then, a fourth step that leads to responsible self-management. It is what might be called, appropriately, spiritual exposure. Sherwood Eddy's description of the spiritual saga of Sir Gordon Guggisberg is suggestive. Sir Gordon was a Canadian of Swiss descent. He was strikingly handsome, played cricket exceptionally well, and was a brigadier general. He was divorced from his wife because of his own unfaithfulness. He served his country through the First World War with unique dedication and loyalty. It was his habit to shave daily before a mirror on which he placed a card bearing the motto, "For God, for King, for Country." He said, "God meant nothing to me, the King meant a little, the Country everything."[8] After the war he became governor of the Gold Coast in Africa. One day a gallant Christian said earnestly to the governor: "You love your country because you have served it all your life; you have taken every opportunity of seeing the king; but you have never sought or even wished to know God." When Guggisberg asked how one could know God, his friend replied: "Some of us believe that Jesus of Nazareth knew more of God than any other man, so we put aside some time each morning to study his thought of God, and to let his Father speak to us, which He will do if Jesus told us the truth about Him." Guggisberg replied, "Damn it! I'll try. It's worth it if it's true." Six months later he was a great Christian, and through the succeeding years he gave his life to the service of the Africans, whom he came to love. He founded a system of higher education for his people and became the most progressive governor in all Africa. He died a poor man because he had given all his possessions to help his people.

The will power in Guggisberg was in his willingness to expose himself to the highest as he saw it in Jesus Christ. The conquest of the menace in the man was God's doing. It was God's response to the quest of man, God's answer to the need of Guggisberg.

We cannot find the power of the Highest to manage and control our lives unless and until we expose ourselves to Him and learn to love Him as Guggisberg did. But to expose ourselves to His life, His message, His spirit, is to love Him. Obviously we cannot love Him without knowing Him and we cannot know Him without exposing ourselves to Him in study and meditation and worship. The miracle of what Paul called "newness of life" and power to manage the self creatively is a mystery until we answer our own doubt in terms of Philip's advice to Nathaniel, "Come and see."

The fifth step toward responsible self-management is a corollary to the fourth. It is faith to believe profoundly in the great imperatives of character revealed in and through the Master. It is the emerging certainty that truth and beauty, goodness and love are not electives in the university of life but are its ultimate requirements for graduation. These are values to which we give obedience, no matter what pleases us at the moment. Honesty is not just the best policy; it is the only policy. Concern for the welfare of others is not a matter of expedience; it is a moral necessity. Love is not simply a possible alternative to hate; it is a compelling demand imposed by the love of God.

The great imperatives voluntarily accepted as expressions of

love for the highest are beyond us and yet within us. By that I
mean that they are the ultimate demands of God's universe,
and yet they live in us. An old gentleman, very deaf, expressed
the idea neatly when he put a decisive end to an argument by
turning off his hearing aid to thwart the opposition and then
remarking with pointed finality: "Truth is what has got itself
believed by me." The old man was at least half right. Truth,
to do you any good, must be believed by you, cherished by you.
Imperatives, to mean anything to you, must be believed in and
honored by you. But when truth is believed and loved by you
and the imperatives have been embraced by you, nothing can
shake the foundations on which you stand.

Despite the menace in you and the circumstances that threaten
your inner integrity, when you believe in the great imperatives
revealed in Jesus and stand by them, they will stand by you
and hold you steady, as Rudyard Kipling made clear in the
story of Kim. Kim was an English lad reared in India. The
boy's adventures were fabulous and the story is enchanting. A
series of events led Kim to the home of Lurgan Sahib of the
British Secret Service. Lurgan needed a lad with a good head.
But he needed to be sure of Kim, so after Kim had quenched
his thirst from an earthen jar, Lurgan commanded him to
throw the jar to the floor. "But," Kim objected, "it will break."
"I say, throw it," Lurgan urged. Kim pitched the jar. It fell
and crashed into fifty pieces. "I said it would break," Kim
murmured. But Lurgan, using his hypnotic powers, sought to
cast a spell on Kim. "All one, look at it," he said. Gently
stroking the nape of Kim's neck, Lurgan went on, "Look, it
shall come to life again, piece by piece."

To save his life, Kim could not have turned his head. The
jar, smashed before his eyes, seemed to be coming together.
"Look, it's coming into shape," Lurgan purred. Kim shook
himself, trying to resist the hypnotic spell, and his mind took

refuge in the multiplication table. "It's coming into shape," Lurgan repeated. "Twice three equals six," Kim said to himself, "and three times three is nine, and four times three is twelve." Kim clung desperately to the repetition. The shadow outline of the jar cleared like a mist lifting. "Three times twelve is thirty-six." "Look, it's coming into shape?" Lurgan's statement was a question. "No, it is smashed," Kim gasped, free from the spell that had almost engulfed his mind.

Kim saved himself by clinging to the truths he knew were true. Two times three is six and three times three is nine. No matter what illusions threatened to swamp his mind, these things were true and sound. So when times are out of joint and what you see around you seems to challenge all you have believed, cling to the truths you know are true; stand by the imperatives and they will stand by you. Not long ago I received a letter from a young man in an Army camp. "I am with a group of men whose ideals and standards clash with mine," he wrote. "By everything they do they seem to say I'm crazy. Sometimes I wonder if I am, and then I think of Jesus Christ and I feel sure again." Two times three is six and God's imperatives revealed in Christ are sound. One truth is as certain as the other.

The road to responsible self-management is a rugged one, but if we dare to follow it until the great imperatives revealed in Jesus Christ become the lode-stars of our striving and our seeking, life will find meaning in its sure direction and we will lay the foundations for a faith with which to manage our lives.

CHAPTER II

Get Rid of Your Guilt

YOUR problem of managing yourself is complicated by an accumulation of memories that leave your mind as cluttered as your grandmother's attic. Some lovely antiques are there, growing more precious with the passing years. But there also is an accumulation of refuse that ought to be thrown out forthwith. Guilt, like a tattered lace curtain, lies in a dark corner, a fire hazard in the mind as in an attic. Sins, swept out of sight, like fragments of a broken jar pushed behind an empty box, are ever present reminders of something needing to be done. What is worse, the clutter keeps piling up year after year as we postpone the inevitable cleaning process.

Now and then the problem becomes acute. Spontaneous combustion in some unswept corner threatens the whole house. The cluttered mind infects the body, or perhaps besets the nerves. The conflagration threatens sanity or health. Sometimes the reasons for our shattered nerves or shattered health are hidden even from ourselves. And yet,

> . . . when the body's sick and ill at ease,
> The mind doth often share in the disease.

Perhaps more often it is the mind that inspires the disease, for hidden guilt is like a poison spreading through the system, needing to be localized and drained.

Sleeping pills and aspirin help us not at all, as a woman noted some years ago when she came to my study. She was thin, a trifle bedraggled, and emotionally upset. I had never seen her before, and she opened the conversation by saying: "I have been to three doctors and they have no idea what is the matter with me. They don't know what's wrong, but I do." "That's interesting," I said. "What is the matter with you?" "Well," she said, "I have been having an affair with a man who is not my husband and I can't stand myself any more. It is driving me crazy."

Obviously the woman was both nervously distraught and physically ill as a consequence of an unrelieved sense of guilt. She and her husband were buying a house and she was working to help pay off the mortgage. What had begun as a casual office flirtation had developed into a serious affair. After the affair had gone beyond the bounds of propriety, the interlude of moral failure turned into a devastating guilt complex. Retribution came in tension, fear, physical exhaustion, and inner despair. Life turned into dust and ashes and everything seemed wrong. Doctors could not help because their physical remedies could not reach the spiritual root of her problem. Sleeping pills could not help because the dawn brought the agony of remorse. The instinct of the woman was sound when she came to the church for help. The church had meant nothing to her since her childhood, and yet she was aware that her problem was basically spiritual.

"Does your husband know what has been going on?" I asked her. "No," she answered. "Do you think I should tell him?" After some discussion she concluded of her own volition that she never would be free from fear, the fear of discovery, unless she confessed her sin to her husband.

The next day her husband dropped into my study. It was clear that he was suffering from a serious shock. He had not had the slightest suspicion of his wife's unfaithfulness. His first reaction was that there could be no way out except an immediate divorce. After a time, however, he admitted he loved his wife devotedly. I told him a bit of the story of Hosea, of a love that would not surrender no matter what the provocation. He admitted that, for the sake of a small son whom he and his wife both loved deeply, somehow the marriage should be salvaged. He left my office undecided what he would do.

Two days later the woman and her husband both returned. They were holding hands as they entered my study. She told me tearfully that they had decided to go on together, that he had forgiven her and that for the first time in months she felt free. She asked me to pray for God's forgiveness for her and that together she and her husband might build a worthy home. "I want you to know," she said, "that both of us are coming back to church. We have neglected our religion much too long and from now on we are going to keep close to God because only God can keep us together." Shortly after that episode I moved to another church and it was three years later that I had a letter, a joyous letter of gratitude. The woman and her husband had moved to another town, started again, and together they had built a happy home and a successful marriage. "Which is easier," Jesus asked, "to say, 'Your sins are forgiven,' or to say 'Rise . . . and walk'?"[1]

A gnawing sense of guilt unrelieved by a great forgiveness is both physically and spiritually devastating. It leaves us ill physically and ill emotionally. Frequently it drives us to alcoholism in a wild effort to escape the haunting memories that will not leave us alone. Some times it sends us hurrying relentlessly through the days in endless activity to submerge the temptation to think and to brood. We seek to lose ourselves in crowds because it is hell to be alone. Yet dark thoughts peek through the cracks in our crowded days.

There always is the fear of discovery that follows us in our waking and troubles us in our sleep. Our hearts pound furiously when the truth about us trembles over the abyss of discovery. If we cannot bear the tension we crack and the mind retreats into the elysium of irrationality. When reality is too difficult to bear, the mind finds surcease in the make-believe of unreality. It does not matter, then, who knows the truth. We are not responsible by reason of insanity, temporary or otherwise. In the world of irrationality there is no longer any reason to be afraid.

If the mind does not crack the days are full of misery, as if some demon pursued us. Cain felt the ominous truth when, after the murder of his brother, he wandered over the face of the earth complaining: "My punishment is greater than I can bear."[2] A troubled man, haunted by fear that his embezzlement of funds would be discovered, opened a conversation with the words, "I can't stand it any longer." Our sins punish us with a sense of guilt and with the terrifying fear that what we have done will come to light. Anxious days follow anxious days until we wonder if there is any point to going on. Life has no meaning except the meaning of flight, of running away faster and faster.

But fear is only one of the legacies of sin that turn inexorably into a sense of guilt. There is also the turbulence of inner conflict, with the self quarreling with the self, the "is" ranged against the "ought to be." We cannot escape from the compulsion of what ought to be, relentlessly condemning what we are and do. We are at war with ourselves and yet we are constrained to live with ourselves day after day and year after year. Guilt devastates the kingdoms of the mind and of the emotions until we hate ourselves. Then the stresses of the world around us become more than we can bear. As Axel Munthe notes in *The Story of San Michele,* "A man can stand a lot as long as he can stand himself. He can live without hope, without books, without friends, without music as long as he can listen to his own thoughts."[3] We are done, however, if we cannot endure the nature of our own thoughts. If we are tortured by remorse, distressed by unrelieved guilt, haunted by the specter of life as it might have been, the strain of meeting the world is too much to bear.

"The kingdom of God is within you,"[4] but so is the kingdom of torment. "I myself am heav'n and hell"[5] was Omar Khayyám's way of saying that the memories that people our minds are the final arbiters of peace or conflict within. Our guilty memories drive us into self-made hells, as John Milton understood when he wrote,

> The mind is its own place, and in itself
> Can make a heaven of hell, a hell of heaven.[6]

Our guilt takes the joy from the joyous and robs the days of their possible richness. Our dividedness turns even the most promising adventure into a misery and a regret.

Again, guilt robs life of its essential meaning. We were born to fulfill our moral and spiritual possibilities, to win the glory of the lighted mind. We were meant to achieve "the moral grandeur of independent integrity." We were intended for fellowship with God. But in our weakness we miss the royal road to life as it was meant to be. We blunder into lostness without a sense of moral direction or spiritual destination. Our guilt fouls the compass of our souls and we wander without knowing whither we go or why.

In a sense, our experience is akin to that of Admiral Byrd during his first stay on Little America. He was alone in the long night that had settled over the bottom of the world, and he had left his snow cave to examine the meteorological instruments which were to provide valuable information about

the land of everlasting snow. Since there always was danger
of getting lost, he had taken the precaution of establishing a
life line of bamboo sticks set in the snow. He would walk back
and forth along the line of sticks.

One night the Admiral walked beyond the line of sticks
without realizing it. Suddenly he sensed his danger and turned
in the direction where he thought he would find his life line.
He traveled one hundred paces, but he found no bamboo sticks.
Then there came over him, he wrote, "a sinking, sickening
sensation," and he whispered to himself, "Now you're lost."
Happily he kept his head and carefully and thoughtfully ex-
plored the terrain until he discovered the line of sticks and
retraced his steps to his snow cave.

Now and then we wander beyond the life-line imperatives,
the truths we know are true and the rights we know are right,
and in a "sinking, sickening" moment a sense of guilt descends
upon us and we know that we are lost, wandering in the waste-
land. Yet we know the great imperatives are there to guide us
toward inner security. The "moral law within" is as inevitable
as "the starry heavens above." Can we find the imperatives and
cherish them again when our sense of guilt blots out the stars
like a fog? Can we find the way home to the security of re-
newed integrity? We wonder in our lostness.

Perhaps the most devastating aspect of a sense of guilt is the
feeling of isolation it begets. It separates us from both God and
man. It separates us from our fellow men as an unpaid grocery
bill separates us from the grocer. The bill is a problem to the
grocer but it is a deeper problem for the man who owes the
bill. The grocer may be understanding and fair, but the man
who owes a long-standing bill feels uncomfortable, guilty.
When he sees the grocer at a lodge meeting or even in the
church he is ill at ease. He avoids meeting the grocer if he can
manage it. But the barrier between the grocer and himself is in

his own mind and conscience far more than it is in the grocer.

So a sense of guilt separates us from the sinned against and often from others as well. We suspect, rightly or wrongly, that the world around us is aware of the guilt we feel within. Suspicion and uneasiness plague our days and drive us from sustaining comradeships. We are like a man I know who moved to another town and tried to start again because he could not face the friends he feared might know the secret of his own heart. But the new town was no better than the town he left. He could not leave his guilt behind. Still he felt his isolation from the world.

But there is more. Guilt separates us from God, even as it isolates us from friends. The love of God is steady as the stars, but we remove ourselves from it. We close the door upon ourselves, and though He stand at the door and knock, we leave it closed. We seem to pray to heavens of brass whose echoes still accuse our guilt. We burn with shame and feel the weight of something wrong within. We have no sense of contact with the source of life and hope. The end is despair and hell inside.

Inevitably we try to escape from our guilt before we are willing to come to terms with it and seek creative ways out of it. Normally we seek escape in one of three ways. First, we attempt to reduce our standards. We tell ourselves, "We can't be perfect" so we may as well do as the Romans do with a good conscience. There really is no use trying to be moral Phi Beta Kappas. Good enough is good enough. So, with the Kinsey reports to undergird us, we decide sex may as well be a casual thing. What is the use worrying about purity? In a sense we excuse our sins by sneering at our aspirations.

The difficulty is that the imperatives remain. The Ten Commandments are still the Ten Commandments even though we revise them in our own illusory interests. The highest values of human experience remain the highest even if we reject them for our own convenience. Take, for example, the Christian ideal of one man and one woman loving each other and living together "until death us do part." It involves problems of discipline and faith, but it holds life's greatest promise. It is valid even though we reject it in the interests of marathon marriage. Trial marriage is more or less commonplace, to be sure, and if you do not like the sample you can try again, and again if need be.

The question is, is the contemporary pattern of married behavior more ultimately good than the "old-fashioned" habit of sticking together through thick and thin, meeting problems and conflicts and issues in the presence of God and giving obedience to His imperatives? I thought of that question once when I had luncheon with an eighty-three-year-old man who has been living with the same lady for fifty-three years. Laughingly he remarked, "She's an eighteen-eighty-two model, but I wouldn't trade her." He went on to say, "We've had our ups and downs, but we've raised a wonderful family and I'm a grateful and a happy man."

We do not really escape from anything, certainly not from a sense of guilt, when we simply lower our standards to meet the needs of our morals. Sooner or later we will come across somebody who took the high road, and then the low road we traveled will seem shoddy beyond measure. It may be too late, then, to recover the glories of life that might have been, and guilt and regret will have their day.

Closely linked to the disposition to lower our standards to meet the needs of our morals is the will to deny that sin is sin because there really are no standards with any authority to guide our lives. Irving Shaw pictures the mood in his striking story, "The Troubled Air," in which Vic, a Communist, is busy undermining the foundations of our beloved land. He betrayed his best friend on the assumption that loyalty is a bourgeois virtue. He practiced deception on a vast scale, as if truth were an unnecessary encumbrance. He destroyed his own home and made light of the love of his wife, as if love were a sign of weakness. He was unimpressed by the claims of the moral law. But life on Communistic terms is scarcely to be justified, even though we adopt the essentials of Communist philosophy in our attempts to escape the sense of guilt. Sin and evil remain sin and evil even though we call them good, and love and integrity continue to be essential virtues even though we describe them as weakness.

It is important to remember that the only unpardonable sin in the New Testament is sin against the Holy Spirit, and sin against the Holy Spirit is simply failure to recognize sin as sin. It is dressing up evil in the robe of righteousness and calling it good. It is doing what you want to do for the sake of expediency or convenience and then calling it good when it is evil. It is rationalizing your selfish interests until you have equated your interests with the will of God. It is stooping to unethical business practices and justifying them because they get results. The unpardonable sin is not corruption, but corruption that ceases to be recognized as corruption because it achieves a political objective the party insists is good.

The Greek word for sin used in the New Testament is *amartia,* and it means "to miss the mark." Anybody can be forgiven for missing the mark, but to miss the mark and then to insist you hit it until you make yourself believe you did is unforgivable. When we do that we are somewhat like the Arkansas hillbilly who went around the countryside shooting at everything he saw. A hunter following his trail was amazed to notice that the young fellow always scored bull's-eyes. He never missed. There would be a chalk circle on the side of a barn or a tree and precisely in the middle a hole where the bullet had hit. When the hunter met the hillbilly he commented on such excellent marksmanship. "Oh, that's easy," said the hillbilly. "I just shoot and then draw a ring around the bullet hole."

You and I have an unholy habit of doing what we want to do and then drawing a ring of righteousness around our conduct. That, says the New Testament, is unforgivable. Some years ago a young woman came to my study with a hint of belligerence. "Can you give me any good reason," she asked, "why I should not have an affair with a married man who works in the office where I work?" "Well," I asked, "what's holding you back?" I thought for a moment I had asked the wrong question. She burst into tears. Then, tearfully, she said: "Everything I ever believed and thought to be right is holding me back. But he says I am a relic of the Victorian era, and I ought to get up to date." There you have a sample of the unforgivable sin. Shooting at what you want and calling it right because you say it is "up to date."

The third means we use to escape our sense of guilt is self-deception. We assume a self-righteous stance on the assumption that others are guilty of a multitude of "sins we have no mind to." Because we are innocent of the so-called cardinal sins, like murder, adultery, and forgery, we whitewash ourselves and conclude we are better than we really are. We excuse our discourtesies on the grounds that at least we did not do violence to anyone. We turn our small lies into virtues because we did not embezzle money from the bank. We call our prejudices sound common sense and our intolerance wisdom because in our circles our prejudices and our intolerance are generally accepted as thoroughly respectable ways of thinking. We deceive ourselves about ourselves and effect a temporary escape from the sense of guilt.

The Pharisees were self deceived. They would not admit their guilt. On the contrary, they saw themselves as defenders of the ancient faith of Israel. Jesus denounced them roundly for their hypocrisy when they brought him the woman taken in adultery, as if his notion of sin and theirs were altogether different. The respectable guardians of the morals of Jerusalem brought the woman half naked before Jesus. No wonder he averted his eyes and wrote in the sand. The Jewish law insisted she should be stoned, and the men who hated Jesus wanted him to condemn her. Adultery was sin. She had been caught in the act; let her be punished according to the law. "Very well," said Jesus, "he that is without sin among you, let him cast the first stone at her."[7] The crowd melted away like ice in a July sun. When only Jesus and the woman were left he asked, "Doth no man condemn thee?" When she shook her head in shame the Master responded: "Neither do I condemn thee: go and sin no more."

Certainly no man was more relentless in his insistence upon marital fidelity than Jesus. He did not condone adultery or any other sins of sex, not for one moment. Nevertheless, he forgave the woman who was guilty of adultery, and there is a tradition which insists that she was none other than Mary Magdalene, who loyally followed Jesus through the years and in the end stood before the empty tomb on Easter morning. If that is true, and I like to think it is, the Master's forgiveness was the beginning of a great redemption.

As Leslie Weatherhead points out, there is a vast difference between what Jesus said to the woman taken in adultery and what he said to the respectable Pharisees. To the woman he said, when no one condemned her: "Neither do I condemn thee: go and sin no more." But listen to this addressed to the respectable leaders of the Jewish community: "You serpents, you brood of vipers, how are you to escape being sentenced to hell?"[8] That was stern, blunt language. It was spoken, mind you, not to the corrupt government officials who swarmed like leeches around Pilate's court, not to the dishonest tax collectors like Zacchaeus, whose thievery was a household complaint, but to the best citizens of Jerusalem.

What were the sins of the best people that warranted the condemnation of Jesus? There was the smug self-righteousness of the Pharisees, and their way of being legally correct but loveless. They exhibited the superiority complex of successful men who worshiped themselves. They fought to preserve the *status quo* because it was good for them, even though others suffered on account of it. They betrayed a loveless cruelty and indifference to human values for the sake of personal profit. They resorted to the hypocrisy of discrediting Jesus by calling him names like "winebibber and glutton" when they could not meet his arguments with logic. They stopped at nothing to undermine the influence of those who stood in their way just to get them out of the way. All the while they hid their guilt behind the robes of respectability. So do we!

No doubt, if you judged your sins the way Jesus judged them you would understand why your life is disordered so often and why you are plagued by restlessness and inner sterility. If you are a business executive and you have been ruthless and un-mindful of human values, you cannot escape your guilt in the presence of the Highest. If you are an employee, you may be under judgment for pretending to be hard at work when you really are loafing on the job. You are guilty before God for deceptions, like pretending that business by cocktail is necessary when actually you simply lack courage to defy what is customary. You are not free from guilt if you have been trying to discredit somebody you did not like by innuendo and gossip. Vindictiveness, selfishness, and refusal to forgive others may be the "respectable" sins that make you guilty before God. What is more, your respectable sins are destroying your "peace of mind" and leaving you a hollow shell without spiritual substance.

Unhappily, we go on indulging in our respectable sins, not knowing precisely why life seems so meaningless because we seldom stop long enough to face our guilt. Once, during wartime, Bishop Gore disturbed his friends at a sumptuous meal by saying, when he was asked to return thanks, "O Lord, forgive us for feasting while others starve." He simply put into words an unfamiliar notion. And yet, the idea lurks in our consciousness, buried beneath the surface and upsetting us in our extravagance. That is why the multiplication of things brings us neither inner satisfaction nor peace of mind.

We cannot escape the consequences of a sense of guilt. Whether we acknowledge it or not, it is there to plague our souls and keep our lives in turmoil. We may lower our standards, deny that sin is sin, or deceive ourselves, but we cannot escape our guilt. We can, however, deal with it creatively if we begin with the honest confession that our sin is sin and no sophistry can make it anything else. The only sin you cannot conquer is the sin you will not admit, and the only sin God cannot forgive is the sin you dress up in the white robes of righteousness. Excuses and self-defense leave you with your sins compounded. Even an unintentional mistake becomes a sin when you try to defend it. But a mistake can turn into a source of strength when you face it fairly. Anybody will forgive an honest mistake honestly confessed, but nobody will forgive an honest mistake when you excuse it or deny it was a mistake.

There was a glorious quality of honesty in Mayor LaGuardia of New York City, who did much to reform a corrupt city. On one occasion he appointed a judge to the municipal bench who turned out to be thoroughly dishonest. When reporters confronted him with the fact that he had appointed a scoundrel to office, Mayor LaGuardia made no effort to justify himself. He accepted the responsibility with the thoroughly honest comment, "Boys, all I've got to say is this: When I make a mistake it's a beaut."

So, at the outset, confess your fault to yourself. Acknowledge the fact of your sin. Admit it to yourself and stop telling yourself you hit the mark when you missed it by a mile or more. You are hopelessly beaten if you go on clinging to your self-deception. Stand yourself up against the wall with Christ and admit to yourself you have betrayed him. Even the best of men have prayed with Wordsworth:

> The best of what we do and are,
> Just God forgive.[9]

Often it is helpful as an affirmation of your own sincerity to confess your sin to someone you trust implicitly—a devoted friend, a minister, a physician. Such confession gets sin and guilt out of the dark and into the light. It brings the light of day to the dark, hidden corners where unwanted cobwebs linger to remind us of unsavory yesterdays. "Confess your sins to one another,"[10] says James. The open confession relieves the inner tension of a cornered conscience and leads to freedom and peace. Without confession, memory often persists in opening doors into the past which we thought we had shut and bolted. Unexpected breezes blow dirt from concealed corners into the middle of the room.

There are those who come to my study now and then because they have been in touch with Alcoholics Anonymous. They want desperately to conquer their alcoholism, and as a beginning they must confess their sins to someone both to affirm their sincerity and to cleanse their minds. They know full well they have retreated into alcohol as a means of escape from something. But their escape led them into sins, sometimes grievous ones. So they drink more to escape the sins in which they are involved. The vicious circle goes on and on until they know they are finished without help. They cannot even begin to fight their way back until they have confessed their sins both to themselves and to another. I recall one man who began his story cautiously, and then suddenly the bars were down and the sordid tale poured out like a pent-up flood. It went on and on until it was all unfolded. When finally he stopped, he put his head on his hands and sobbed, "I feel better than I have for ten years."

Important as confession is, it is only a preliminary to the finding of forgiveness. Paradoxically, you cannot forgive yourself until you have been forgiven. It may be that you make amends to those you have wronged and win their forgiveness. Possibly you cannot. At least you ought to try. One man who had cheated and lied so often he could not remember all those he had wronged set out to make what amends he could, and to ask forgiveness of those he knew he had wronged. The reactions he met varied from gratitude and encouragement combined with forgiveness to downright disbelief and cynical sneers. He took both the forgiveness and the sneers in his stride. He even kept his temper when one man derided him before a crowd with the remark, "Hey, boys, Jim's got religion. Who wants to bet a dollar it is as phony as his last proposition?"

But God never sneers. His love is as steady as the stars. He waits for our repentance with a patience beyond anything we know of patience. He offers His forgiveness and His strength on only one condition: "Go and sin no more!" He accepts you as you are "without one plea" because He loves you with an everlasting love. He was seeking you even when you were unmindful of Him. While you had forgotten Him, He had not forgotten you. You closed the door upon Him. It was not the other way about. When you sought forgiveness in humility and sincerity, you opened the door for His spirit and His power.

Two things need to be said about the forgiveness of God,

however. One is that even the forgiveness of God does not write off all the consequences of sin. As Adam Bede said, "Sin is like a bit o' bad workmanship. You never see the end o' the mischief it will do." But forgiveness makes consequences endurable. It alters relations. Forgiveness mends broken fellowship, and broken fellowship is the most damaging of all the results of sin. We can endure the consequences of sin because we comprehend the justice of the consequences. What we cannot endure is the sense of alienation, of isolation from our fellows and from God. A small boy put the matter in proper perspective when he said to his mother, "Mom, I don't mind being spanked, but please don't look at me that way."

Again, even the forgiveness of God does not automatically inspire perfection. To be sure, it turns life in a new direction, infuses it with new purpose, lifts it to new heights of goodness. But, as John Milton noted, "Long is the way and hard, that out of hell leads up to light."[11] Temptations assail us as long as we live, and we never altogether achieve final security in the good. But the forgiveness of God sets us free to move in new directions. I felt the truth some years ago riding in a railroad coach between Kansas City and St. Louis when a young man sat down beside me. "Are you saved?" he asked me. I was not annoyed, as I sometimes have been by that question. He was obviously sincere and clearly concerned about my spiritual welfare. We talked at some length. What he meant by salvation was clear. He wanted to save me from the tortures of the everlasting, to be sure that when my life was done I would rest securely in the comfort of heaven. But, somehow, I could not follow him there. When he left the train, I found myself asking the question over and over again: "From what am I saved?"

As the train rolled on through Missouri, I wondered: Was I saved from my pride? Not altogether. Are you? Am I saved from my angers? Are you? Am I saved from the sins that make my life less than it might have been, less than it might be? Not altogether. Are you? Nevertheless, I know that I am infinitely better than I might have been because along the road I have paused again and again to find the forgiveness of God. You too can find forgiveness and freedom from the guilt that weighs you down. You can find the great salvation and come closer to the good than you ever have been before.

On the road from festering guilt to spiritual health and creative self-management, forgiveness follows confession, and commitment follows forgiveness. Commit your life to the tides that flow from Calvary's hill. Give yourself to the high purposes and loyalties that stream through the ages from the crystal depths of Galilee. Listen to the summons of the Christ, "Follow thou me," and follow through darkness and through light. Anchor your life to the great imperatives and trust them, even when trust seems costly. Your commitment is the testament of your sincerity.

There can be no halfheartedness, no holding back, in the great commitment of faith. Tapering off won't do the job. You cannot leap a chasm in two jumps. Besides, God is no spare tire for emergencies only. He is no part-time trouble shooter. He is all or nothing. Either you want Him to manage your life or you don't. There is no halfway house. It is fatal to be like the lady who started to climb off a pier into a rowboat and then, after her feet were in the boat, fearfully clung to the pier. As the boat, with her feet in it, drifted out, and her hands clung to the pier, she tumbled into the lake. It is a parable of our religious experience. You cannot plant your feet on the buoyant strength of God and at the same time cling to an egoistic confidence in your ability to manage things your own way. You can't put one hand into the hand of God and with the other hang on to your sins. You stake your faith on God and let go of your pride and your sins or you sink.

One alcoholic, trying to escape the misery of his estate, wanted to know if he could hang on to an illicit love affair and still find God's help in dealing with his alcoholism. The answer is obvious. Either you want God enough to surrender or you don't, and if you won't surrender you can't win. But when you make the great commitment of faith you discover God's strength is able to bear the burden of your weakness and you find life's meaning in your own soul's growth. The "Everlasting Arms" are no mirage, born of wishful thinking. They are the ultimate security of one who dares to say:

> Take my life and let it be
> Consecrated, Lord, to Thee.[12]

Paul knew something about the power of God, flowing from the great commitment. He called it "the power of God for salvation."[13]

When you come to the place where you are soberly aware that for your own soul's sake you must find forgiveness and make a new start, the Gospels have three things to say that put new meaning into your days. They begin by telling you it never is too late to start over with God. The whole of Christian history has been built upon men and women who started life over again. Almost anyone you can mention in the New Testament was somebody who had to turn over a new leaf. The disciples and Paul, Mary Magdalene and Zacchaeus made new beginnings. The great leaders of the church from Augustine to Starr Daily had to get rid of old habits and learn new ones. Paul says the Christian faith means "newness of life," life that is different because Christ has touched it.

Some years ago I had dinner one evening with two men who had gone wrong about as far as any two men could go and then found God and fought their way back. They had lost everything—their reputations, their money, their families. Finally, both of them hit bottom. The world looked so black there was nothing to do but climb back or else stay in a drunken stupor. They came to themselves, then, and resolved to start over with God. That night, as we sat together after dinner, one of the men drew from his pocket a letter he had received the day before from his daughter, away at college. "Daddy," she wrote, "I am happier than you can guess, and wonderfully proud of you. Five years ago I felt lost and hurt and ashamed, but now I am so grateful it actually hurts. Thank you, daddy, for what you have done to make us all proud of you." He wept without shame before he finished reading the letter to us.

The Christian faith insists in the second place that it is never too late to start over with God because God's love never lets go. We say love is blind, and maybe it is when those who love us go on believing in us no matter what we do. But God is blind that way too. He goes on seeing beneath our surface and seeming to what we were meant to be and can be. The truth is suggested by a striking episode in a contemporary novel, wherein an outraged family is trying to persuade a daughter to leave her no-good husband. He has brought nothing but misery and unhappiness to everyone, but, says his loyal wife: "I guess he's no good, but I love him. Maybe if I stick to him he will come to himself. I still believe he is better than he seems."

God said that once to Israel: "How can I give thee up, Ephraim?"[14] Israel seemed to be "no good." The people were running after false gods, making images and scorning the law. The government was corrupt and, as Isaiah said, "the whole head is sick, and the whole heart faint."[15] But God would not give up. He would not let His people go. Nor will He let us go. We may crowd Him out of our lives, ignore His commandments, and live as if we never heard of Jesus, but God will not let us go or turn aside from seeking us. You may wonder sometimes if you are any good in God's eyes. At your best, you are a blundering fool. You are selfish and stubborn and belligerent. Your sins are many and your follies quite numberless. You have been so busy feathering your own nest that you haven't cared much about the Kingdom of God. Maybe you wonder sometimes why God loves you at all. Somebody asked George Bernard Shaw once whom he would pick among the great men and women of the earth to start a new dispensation if he could be Noah in another flood. The old patriarch flashed back: "I'd let them all drown." Well, maybe Shaw would, but God wouldn't.

God keeps loving you with sublime patience. Now and then under the weight of your guilt you discover the love of God revealed in the cross of Christ and find the forgiveness that is life's ultimate freedom. Now and then you take God's hand, perhaps in tears, and find the crowded, wonderful hour of life that marks your turning and redemption. As the Psalmist notes,

> Oh, the bliss of him whose guilt is pardoned,
> And his sin forgiven,
> Oh, the bliss of him whom the Eternal has absolved,
> Whose spirit has made full confession.[16]

Finally, the New Testament makes it clear that it never is too late to make a new start with God because God wants to forgive and redeem. You cannot live through the pageant of Lent and Holy Week without seeing a pageant of sin and suffering and forgiveness with God in the very middle of it. The whole affair means simply that God is involved with you in life as you live it, hurt by your hurts, grieved by your sins, suffering with you in your suffering. Piers Plowman had it right when he asked: "Who suffers more than God?" You cannot love without suffering with and for those you love. What is more, you cannot love and suffer and not wish to forgive. So with God.

Ah yes, love suffers, but love forgives too. Travel back, if you will, along the road to your childhood. Remember that day when you stubbornly did what you were told not to do. You defended yourself vigorously, insisting you did nothing wrong, and there was a disturbing barrier between you and your mother. You knew she was terribly hurt, and inside you knew that you were wrong, but you tried to bluff it through. You went around feeling miserable. The whole world seemed wrong. Then, when you could stand it no longer, you threw yourself into your mother's arms and said: "Mom, I'm sorry. I was wrong." She forgave you, then, because she loved you, and the world that had been so wrong seemed right again. The tension was gone and you could not do enough to make amends. You helped with the chores and did the little things that bring a song to the heart.

You are a grown-up child now, a "child of God," and things seem terribly wrong. You have been trying to bluff, trying to make wrong seem right. Maybe some day you will come to the point where you can stand it no longer and you will say: "O God, I'm sorry. I have been so wrong." You will go out to make amends, then, and God will forgive you. The tension will be gone and the fear. You will want to do the little things that brighten life for others. Yes, your pride will be punctured and the props kicked from under your self-importance. But you will meet the glorious paradox of forgiveness, the loss that turns into gain, the pain that turns into profit.

CHAPTER III

Nobody Needs to Be Nobody

PERSONALITY is full of paradoxes. On one hand, as we saw in the first chapter, the egocentric predicament is a menace to our maturity. On the other hand, the mature self needs to be aware of its significance. Unhappily, in our complex world personality is imperiled by the sense of insignificance. Surrounded by impersonal forces, we feel small and inadequate. In a world of somebodies, we often seem to be nobodies. Nevertheless, one of the deepest psychological urges in human nature is the urge to be a somebody, to be significant. We think life really would mean something if we were somebodies.

In an amusing cartoon a harassed and homely woman is pictured at a cocktail party standing before a mild little man who sits on a settee mopping his brow. In the background a collection of important people in long dresses or white ties and tails are talking and drinking. The woman, with obvious relief, says to the little man: "Oh, it's wonderful to meet somebody who is nobody." That comment suggests a very common feeling. We welcome an escape when we are obscured and overwhelmed by somebodies. We would rather be big fish in little puddles than little fish surrounded by leviathans in a big pond. We are

44

distressed when we feel unimportant among important people, insignificant among the significant.

You and I want to be somebodies. We want recognition from the world around us and some response from those with whom we live and work. Often our desire for importance leads us to sin and guilt. Children, living in an adult world, find themselves overshadowed and often ignored. They react with misbehavior. They would rather be spanked than ignored. They resort to all manner of ruses from tantrums to tears to gain attention. Adults are like children. Beauty parlors thrive on our adult craving for recognition and approval. Like children we indulge in all sorts of subterfuges to gain attention.

Lyle E. Dougherty adopted a unique means of gaining attention and becoming important.[1] He bought a watch wholesale. Presently word got around that Dougherty, a studious, bespectacled, mild-mannered man, could "get it for you wholesale." Soon his co-workers were besieging him with requests to buy television sets, electrical appliances, and even cars for them. "It made me very popular," Dougherty recalled, "and I hated to refuse." Even executives of the Briggs Manufacturing Company in Detroit heard about Dougherty, the man "who can get it for you wholesale." They, too, began bombarding him with orders. He had become important, a somebody to everybody.

Unfortunately, Dougherty never really succeeded in getting anything wholesale—except that first watch. He had to pay retail prices "and then deliver the articles at a good discount, paying the difference himself." He spent every nickel of his savings. He borrowed from finance companies and banks. It was no use. He was too popular. Finally Dougherty's world caved in. A friend who had given him $250 as a deposit to buy a new car complained to police that Dougherty had never delivered it. The Wayne County Prosecutor's Office investigated and discovered that Dougherty had collected $121,000 to buy things wholesale and had spent $151,000 on them. He was still $12,655 in debt. At Recorder's Court, where Dougherty pleaded guilty to obtaining money under false pretenses, psychiatrists gave him a going over. "A typical ego-satisfaction, which, probably unknowingly, he valued more than money." So, to win recognition, "a place in the sun," Dougherty played the good fellow and got himself in jail.

Maybe we avoid the extremes that lead us to the folly of Lyle Dougherty, but we have our ways of gaining attention. C. Parker notes significantly that "The most notable inferiority-compensation in industrial life is the strike." The coal strike that brings the nation to its knees gives the individual coal miner a new sense of his own importance. Maybe he is ignored and looked down upon as an insignificant toiler in the bowels of the earth, but he is important. The world cannot move without him. He is somebody, and that fact means far more to him than a few dollars more in his pay envelope.

Social unrest frequently stems from the urge to be somebody. When Napoleon, meditating on the significance of the French Revolution, remarked that "Vanity made the revolution; liberty was only the pretext," he put his finger on a truth of the utmost importance. The depressed and enslaved masses suddenly decided to be somebodies, to claim "a place in the sun." So in our time the vanity of men everywhere is asserting itself. In India a people threw off the yoke of Englishmen who behaved like superiors, and in Iran the people challenged the dominance of the British. The Iranians would rather endure economic chaos than lose face in their struggle. The Communist purges in the Soviet Union were far more a psychological than an economic or political necessity. By liquidating the somebodies, getting rid of the intellectuals and the leaders of the old order, the new leaders established their own importance. They became somebodies. Their intellectual or moral superiors were all dead.

What Wayland Vaughan calls "The Lure of Superiority" is

at once a source of human dynamic and a major peril. It is the
drive of ambition. It makes us want to "keep up with the
Joneses" or get ahead of them if we are able. It drives us into
debt to put on a show of affluence, whether we can afford it or
not. It makes us condescending toward those who occupy
lower rungs on the ladder of worldly success. It breeds conflict
between the haves and have-nots and keeps society in turmoil.
It undercuts our moral principles by raising economic superiority
to the status of the primary value. T. S. Eliot puts the truth
bluntly in *The Cocktail Party.* There the uninvited guest remarks:

> Half of the harm that is done in this world
> Is due to people who want to feel important . . .
> They don't mean to do harm—but the harm does not interest them,
> Or they do not see it, or they justify it
> Because they are absorbed in the endless struggle
> To think well of themselves.[2]

Our human tragedy is that we rest our importance on outward props rather than on inward values. We compensate for
our inward inadequacies by seeking outward recognition. Edna
Ferber points to the truth of the matter in her revealing auto-
biography. In the early days of her career she wrote the highly
entertaining McChesney stories, but she tells us she had a terrific
inferiority complex "which made me feel that all other writers
were superior to me."[3] Since she did not believe in herself, she
felt she needed bolstering. Someone would say with sincerity:
"I like your McChesney stories. They're great." And she would
reply: "Oh, do you really? I thought that last one was quite
bad. I don't know anything about traveling salesmen, anyway.
It wasn't about anything really." By discounting her own stories,
Edna Ferber encouraged other people to bolster her ego. One
way or another she needed social praise to compensate for a
sense of inferiority.

You and I know the mood, for it is ours. "What a lovely

hat," someone says. "Oh, this old thing! It is last year's and I bought it at a sale." "Blue is becoming to you," someone remarks, and you reply, "Don't you think it makes me look a bit sallow?" "That was a fine address you made," some enthusiastic listener observes, and you answer: "I thought it was a bit weak. I could not seem to say what I wanted to say." It is sheer deception, a means of prying compliments from people to sustain an uncertain ego. We build so much on sand, rear our lives and our importance upon the dubious recognition of our fellows. We are utterly deflated by criticism, left with nothing but dust and ashes if we wear a new dress and nobody mentions it or preach a sermon and nobody comments favorably on our effort.

Pearl Buck pictures a modern business tycoon, owner of a chain of newspapers, who is the master of all he surveys. He has a contempt for people and yet a terrible inferiority complex. He wants assurance somehow, somewhere, that everything he is doing is precisely as it should be. He hates his mild and yet successful brother-in-law, Clem, who, with his compassion for people, undermines William's confidence in himself. He finds refuge and security in a Catholic Bishop who, with an eye to the needs of his parish, assures William that everything he is doing is altogether right! Nothing need be changed! And yet, no outward prop, not even a Bishop, can save him from his own inner uncertainty. His closing meditation is revealing:

> What if he had always been wrong? The vague shape of victory—was it he? Or was it Clem? His imagination, diseased and tortured by his soul's perpetual uncertainty, lifted Clem from the grave, brought him back to life, cloaked him in the dark garments of doubt and fear.[4]

Not even wealth and power could save William, or us, or provide enduring significance. Not even the assurance of a Bishop could make up for William's inner insecurity and doubt.

Somebody, like Clem, is forever kicking the secular props of our importance from under us and leaving us devastated. Quite possibly we become neurotic. As Dr. Karen Horney notes, the predominant characteristic of a neurotic is the "excessive dependence upon the approval or affection of others."⁵ When approval is withdrawn and criticism takes its place, the neurotic goes to pieces. Life becomes a long headache on a noisy street, and overwhelming self-pity floods his soul. Take away recognition and approval, success and power, and there is nothing in the inward man or woman to sustain life. The outward props are perilous substitutes for inner spiritual values. Nevertheless, as Jesus suggested, we are forever building our houses on sand, and when storms come, our houses fall. Possibly we put up a front and swagger, or assume an "I don't care" attitude, but inwardly we are miserable. We are walking shadows, without inner substance!

When outward props fail us, we frequently save face by magnifying our difficulties. There is a striking story in the Old Testament which suggests what happens when life rests on outward props. The Children of Israel had been wandering in the wilderness since Moses had led them from their bondage in Egypt. Convinced that they were the "chosen people," they felt strongly that they should be masters, not slaves. They were superior people and they ought to rule and not be ruled. But they were discouraged. They had hoped for so much, and so little had come of their hopes.

The mood of Israel is suggested in the report of the spies who went from the wilderness of Paran to Canaan to "spy out the land" they hoped someday to possess. There were twelve spies, representatives of the twelve tribes of Israel. Evidently they made an extensive journey through the Promised Land, and they found it rich with pomegranates and figs. After forty days they returned to Moses and Aaron to make their report. They admitted quite frankly that the land of Canaan was worthy of their dreams. Truly it was a "land flowing with milk and honey." But they had met the Hittites, the Jebusites, and the Amorites, who were living on the land, and conquest seemed to them quite out of the question. What the spies said, however, suggests that the Hittites, Jebusites, and Amorites were far less significant barriers to Israel's progress than Israel's own state of mind.

The spies insisted that the possessors of the Promised Land were "giants," dwelling in fortified cities. Reading their report one gathers the impression that all the Canaanites were Goliaths of forbidding size and strength. The spies, however, gave themselves away when they added: "We were in our own sight as grasshoppers, and so were we in their sight."[6] Only two of the twelve dared to speak with courage, and one of them, Caleb, "stilled the people before Moses, saying, "Let us go up at once and possess the land; for we are well able to overcome it." But Caleb and Joshua plus Moses made little impression upon the people. They believed the worst and in despair they wailed through the night, "Would that we had died in the land of Egypt." The story would be quite unimportant except for the fact that in our own personal thinking we are so much like the Children of Israel. Modern psychologists probably would say the Children of Israel were suffering from an inferiority complex. Certainly the report of the spies suggests as much. Notice how they magnified their problem and minimized their resources. They insisted that in the Promised Land "we saw . . . giants." How could they, with their ragged, hungry company, march against giants? They didn't have a chance.

The comment of the spies is a remarkable illustration of face-saving. By magnifying their difficulties they would excuse their failures. In a round-about way the spies wanted to convey the idea that the Children of Israel could match the skill and strength of ordinary men, but nobody would expect them to challenge giants. Actually, of course, the Hittites, the Jebusites, and the Amorites were not giants. They were as ordinary as the Children of Israel. Nevertheless, if the inhabitants of Canaan could be raised to the stature of giants, the fears and weaknesses of the Children of Israel would seem altogether justified. The Children of Israel could easily convince themselves that they merely were being prudent when they refused to undertake the impossible.

What the spies did was to provide an alibi for inertia. Of course, they were not unique. They were very much like all of us. We magnify our difficulties until they become towering obstacles we would be fools to challenge. Dr. A. Whitney Griswold, president of Yale University, noted in a commencement address that we have abandoned our political responsibilities as individuals on the assumption that we are quite helpless against the tides that are running in our time. We are excusing inaction and saving face by magnifying our problem. Nobody wants to be nobody, so we preserve our dignity by pleading impossible circumstances; we cannot defeat giants, we say.

Look into your own soul and answer this question for yourself: How many times have you refused a challenge because you magnified the difficulties you would be required to overcome? There is a book you did not write, not because you could not, but because you magnified the limitations of time, the demands of your daily tasks, into impossible barriers to creative achievement. There is the family conflict you did not resolve, not because you could not, but rather because you made difficulties into impossibilities. There is the dishonorable business practice you know you ought to challenge, but you do not. You have saved your self-respect by insisting you cannot change the system. It is a giant. If you make the difficulties great enough you can justify your own weakness. That is what the Children of Israel did when they turned back to the wilderness complaining that the inhabitants of Canaan were giants.

It is important to observe, however, that when the Children of Israel magnified their difficulties they also of necessity minimized their resources. That inevitably happens when you get into the habit of magnifying your difficulties. At first you see the difficulties as a means of excusing your weakness, and then before you know what is happening you lose faith in your own significance. Maybe you become like the lady in Cowper's poem,

> . . . a sad
> And silent cypher, while her proxy plays.[7]

When your magnified problems become an excuse for inertia, you sterilize the resources of mind and spirit that are locked in you. Psychologists tell us that normally we use only 10 per cent of our potential capacities. Your talents may be meager, but you are using only one-tenth of them. It is only a matter of simple arithmetic to say that you can multiply yourself by ten if you can get out of yourself the powers and possibilities that are in you.

The Gospels suggest repeatedly in one way or another that we never really know what resources are imprisoned in our souls until we lose ourselves for the sake of something that gives meaning to effort and lures our hidden powers to the surface. Back in 1879, for example, a Jewish child was born. He was the son of a poor merchant and in early life he suffered a haunting sense of inferiority because of the anti-Semitic feeling he met on every side. Shy and introspective, he was so slow in learning that his parents had him examined by specialists to see if he was normal. He failed his entrance examinations when he tried to enter the Polytechnicum in Zurich, Switzerland, in 1895. He was successful a year later, and at the age of twenty-three he received his doctor's degree at the University of Zurich. After tutoring for a few years he accepted an obscure job as a patent examiner in the Bern patent office. Then an idea seized him.

He called it "relativity." With the dawn of the idea Albert Einstein forgot himself and gave himself to his great idea. Neither he nor anyone else knew what resources of mind were his until he lost himself for an idea that challenged him. He was an illustration of the text: "He that loses his life . . . will find it."[8]

God has given you resources you know not of. Never minimize them. Obviously, when we consider ourselves we need to be essentially honest. It is clear that we are not all equal, but nobody needs to be nobody. There are men of many talents and there are men of few talents. As St. Paul noted, "Now there are varieties of gifts,"[9] but we all have gifts. Not one of us is without resources with which to serve the world creatively. No man needs to be a "silent cypher" while some proxy plays the giant. What is more, you may be sure there is more in you than you ever have gotten out of yourself. God's gifts of mind and spirit in you are greater than you have yet imagined. Walt Whitman got to the heart of the matter when he asked himself: "Walt, you contain enough, why don't you let it out?"[10]

Quite possibly you are not a Phi Beta Kappa and maybe your native talents are altogether ordinary. You cannot compete with Miss America and you have to wear clothes you can afford and hats that come from the bargain basement. You think it is not fair. Other women have all the advantages and you are so ordinary you have no chance at all. More and more you retreat into yourself. In due time you do a fine job of making yourself into a "sad and silent cypher." In all probability you are bitter and resentful. You are discouraged and you feel inferior. Others can do so much that you cannot!

All of us blunder into moments of resentful discouragement and feelings of inferiority. Even the giants have their bad moments of doubt and uncertainty. No matter who you are, there will be days when you feel inside there is something you lack.

Some time ago on a June Sunday morning my church was full at the morning service and I went home rather pleased. The next morning, however, I read a story about Bushman, the famous gorilla. Bushman was very ill, and on that same Sunday he had a congregation. Believe it or not, 120,000 people went to see Bushman that day. He did not have to say a word. He just sat in his cage and nursed his indisposition. God and I drew one thousand on Sunday morning, and Bushman on his own drew 120,000. I struggled with that for a few moments. What did Bushman have that I did not have? Should I give up preaching—a grasshopper among secular giants?

Absurd, you say. Of course it is absurd. Bushman, God rest his gorilla soul, was a 500-pound lummox who could not add two and two. He never paid a tax in his life, and he could not read Shakespeare. I can add two and two. I pay taxes and I read Shakespeare. So while Bushman had something I did not have, I have something Bushman never had. Why should I give up preaching and lament the fact that Bushman could outdraw me 120 to one? So what? I can sing a hymn and Bushman could not!

Quite possibly Susie is beautiful and you are not, but it is altogether possible you can cultivate a quality of spirit and a depth of faith Susie cannot match. Bill may have a million-dollar personality while you are somber and dull, but you may have the stability and persistence Bill lacks. Your neighbor may be a social leader and all you can manage is a little time now and then for the P.T.A., but you may have human insight and understanding your neighbor does not possess. Superiority and inferiority are altogether relative. Let it be noted, too, that when the Children of Israel gave up the notion that the Canaanites were giants, they conquered the Promised Land. When they got over the idea that they were grasshoppers and decided they really were children of God they did what they thought they never could do.

Nobody needs to be nobody, but our importance does not rest upon our position or upon any of the secular social props we so commonly depend upon. Paradoxically, our importance is dependent upon our awareness of the greatness of God. Our significance hinges upon our capacity to see ourselves in the light of God's greatness and goodness. The preacher who conducted the funeral service for Louis XIV in Notre Dame caught the meaning of life in a phrase. The cathedral was gorgeously decorated. Beauty, social distinction, high rank, and political power had crowded into it. The pomp and circumstance of a proud and glittering age had met to honor the king who had been the symbol of the times. Sophisticated, "superior" men and women sat back to listen to the eulogy the preacher was expected to utter. But the preacher's words fell with an icy chill: "Only God is great." Men and women who had come to witness and to share in a spectacle of human pride found themselves confronting God. In a moment of time their worldly importance was stripped away and they were in the presence of God with nothing but themselves.

Kick away all the props to your pride—your house and lot, your automobile, your position, your achievements—and for a moment see yourself a refugee, leaving everything behind but yourself. What do you have left? You have nothing but you, you and the God who alone is great. Possibly the Children of Israel needed exile and disaster and hardship and hurt to sweep away the props to pride before God could offer a solid foundation for their souls. They would not depend upon God until they had nothing else upon which to depend. They could not really believe in God until they had ceased to believe so much in themselves. But in the hours of their deepest need for something to sustain their shattered self-respect they knew that

"Only God is great." Suffering as they were because of their inability to cope with their world, they discovered that "The Lord is my Shepherd" and in their new-found faith they found themselves.

When we know that "Only God is great" we shift the center of our being from ourselves to God, and we begin to ask a new question. Instead of "What do I want?" we begin to ask, "What ought I to want?" We know very well what we do want: position, wealth, power, recognition, "a place in the sun." But what ought we to want? By the light of God's greatness we know we ought to want the hidden values of the soul: integrity and goodness, lasting truth and beauty, and fellowship with God. We ought to want unselfishness and humility, love and something of the mind of Christ. What is more, when the sober fact that "Only God is great" has become a motivating conviction we do begin to want what we ought to want.

Inevitably when in faith and reverent trust we do confess that "Only God is great" we revise our estimate of success and find a new source for our significance. Our importance, then, does not rest upon the secular props we have gathered to sustain our lives, does not depend upon the secular place we hold. God is not interested in your income! He does not care in the least if you are president of the Ancient Order of Cyclops! He does not give you a merit badge because you are a senator or minister of the biggest, brightest church in town. He does not add a pearl to your crown just because everybody in your social set fawns at your feet and thinks you are wonderful.

There is a striking bit of insight into our secular predicament in Samuel Johnson's lines

> The drama's laws the drama's patrons give,
> For we that live to please, must please to live[11]

and yet the lines altogether miss the deeper question upon which spiritual survival and lasting significance depend. Jesus did not live to please nor did he please to live. Indeed, he lives as Lord because he did not please. He lived as he knew he ought to live and displeased the secular giants of his day because he knew he ought to displease them. His importance as a person did not rest upon the approval of Pilate or the Pharisees or the Scribes. His significance hinged upon his obedience to the inner imperatives of God.

Those who led the riotous demonstration against a Negro G.I. in Cicero, Illinois, when he moved into a white neighborhood had the approval of the mob. They were somebodies and they gloried in their importance. No doubt they found a spurious ego-satisfaction in their exploit, but though they pleased the mob no end, they offended God, and "Only God is great." Their success was a thing of rags and tatters, a puny gesture of defiance to the Great and Good. So long as "Only God is great" there is no greatness without goodness, no human importance without some hint in it of the mind of Christ.

Significance, as God sees it, is not measured in terms of approval or accomplishments either. Somebody once described a very superficial debutante as "a well-dressed bundle of accomplishments." The phrase suggests an episode in a discerning novel called *Mink on Weekdays*. Mother believed in "advantages" for young girls. The upshot was that Felicia complained to her cousin, Pat, "Some plants need a lot of water, but there's such a thing as drowning a tender shoot and that's what they're doing to me." To which Pat replied: "There's such a thing as having to submit to so many privileges that you wind up underprivileged."[12] So it is. There is such a thing as feeding so much upon privileges, advantages, and secular accomplishments that you wind up a spiritual vacuum, empty of all enduring significance.

Very wisely Abraham Lincoln put the emphasis of his life in the proper place. He knew that Horace Greeley and a host of others were poking fun at his social awkwardness. He might have learned the intricacies of etiquette had he been interested in pleasing people with social niceties. Lincoln, however, was too sincere to pretend to a culture he did not possess. He was content to be himself, knowing that "outward grace is nothing." As Wayland Vaughan says:

Confident that the task of polishing himself was a hopeless one, he turned to refining the inner man. . . . If he was careless in his attire, it was because his mind was absorbed in matters of greater importance. He knew that people would forgive him his crudity and awkwardness as soon as they learned to appreciate his keen mind, his warm heart, his love of justice, his sense of honor. The grace of sincerity seemed more important to him than training in small talk and sweeping bows. His heart told him that he would be estimated in the long run, not on the basis of his manners, but rather on the basis of his spiritual strength— and he was right.[13]

Lincoln judged himself and his success in terms of his conviction that "Only God is great."

The Gospels insist repeatedly that your significance, your importance as a person, and your worth are altogether independent of anything that appears on the surface. Comparison in measurable externals means nothing in the economy of God. Remember that the Pharisees refused to accept Jesus as Messiah because he would not lead them to a measurable political triumph. "My kingship," he said, "is not of this world."[14] As Jews, they thought of themselves as God's "chosen people," ordained to superiority in the world. Jesus based the Jews' significance as a people and as individuals upon two fundamental spiritual assumptions.

In the first place, they were important because they were worth something to God. They were God's children. Moses tried to make his people see that even in their distress God's care and concern surrounded them. They never could be lost because God would not let them go. He had been "a cloud by day and a pillar of fire by night" to guide them to freedom. He had sustained them with manna and he had preserved them in peril. Nevertheless, all the Children of Israel could see was their utter inadequacy, their futility in the face of odds. God looked upon his people and asked through Moses, "How long will . . . this people not believe in me?"[15]

Never forget that the primary and fundamental premise of the Christian faith is that your significance and your importance as a person rest upon the fact that you are worth something to God. Underneath you are "the everlasting arms." A young man on a submarine instinctively felt the eternal worth of himself when his commander warned him to keep a careful watch for enemy ships. "Don't forget," the commander said, "you're responsible for six million bucks' worth of sub—everything in it—the lives of all of us below." "Yes, sir, Captain," the boy replied, "an' then there's me, too." There's always "me," the essential value in the universe, worth more to God than submarines or the brick and mortar of cities. You may feel unwanted, unneeded, and a bit weary of life. Maybe you can't seem to accomplish much in the world and you feel frightfully inadequate. Well, God does not look upon you as a "sad and silent cypher." "God so loved the world that he gave his only son, that whosoever believes in him should not perish, but have eternal life."[16] The cross of Jesus Christ is God's final pledge that we always are worth something to Him. No man is unimportant if he is loved!

In the second place, your significance hinges upon the fact that God needs what you have to offer, be it much or little. There is a motto I saw somewhere that bears profoundly on the truth. It read: "Without God we cannot; without us God will not." There is work for all of us here, something that needs us terribly. Maybe you can give only love and human understanding to a world full of hate, prejudice, and misunderstanding, "a cup of cold water" to those whose lives are parched. Maybe you can exhibit integrity under strain in a corrupt world, or courage when peril threatens a frightened world. Possibly cheerfulness and courtesy when people are out of sorts are your oblation. Perhaps in your small job you can give an exhibition very quietly of how to do a task the way it ought to be done.

Years ago, Wilberforce Whiteman, whose son, Paul Whiteman, became a distinguished musician, told a story to a class of boys and girls that has stayed with me for forty years. It was the story of a piccolo player in an orchestra. The piccolo seemed frightfully unimportant, playing a line here and there. The violins and the trumpets were important and the drums commanded attention, but the piccolo was just a squeak now and then and nobody noticed it at all. Discouraged, the piccolo player sat disconsolate while the orchestra played. When his lines came, he did not toot. He just sat. A strange look came on the face of the conductor. His fine ear noted something missing. Again the line came that called for notes from the piccolo, and again the instrument was silent. Then, above the roar of the orchestra came the troubled voice of the conductor: "Where's the piccolo?"

The small parts are important. Without them the symphony is incomplete. Nobody needs to be nobody, just playing a small part in the symphony of God. Charles Brookfield, an actor, learned the truth when he was erroneously reported dead. He had the unique opportunity of reading his own obituary. It said, among other things: "Never a great actor, he was invaluable in small parts." "Invaluable in small parts." That is our glory. Most of us are uncommonly common and extraordinarily ordinary, and the small parts are our dish. But we can be invaluable in them. We can be somebodies in the economy of God. I know an elderly widow with nothing much to do, but she voluntarily does mending for the busy mother of three children. She is invaluable in a small part. I know a secretary. Nobody thought she was important until she fell ill, and then it was clear. She was invaluable in a small part.

No matter who you are or what you are doing, God needs you. He needs your hands to serve and your mind for straight thinking. He needs your courage to encourage others, your faith to lift those around you, your integrity to steady your comrades. He needs you to do what would not be done without you; needs you to say what would not be said if you did not say it. You are not a cypher, you are a handle God can use to change the world where you are.

At my summer cottage in the Colorado mountains I have a monkey wrench. I use it just twice a year—once to turn on the water for the house and once to turn it off. If that monkey wrench could think and feel, I suspect it would be discouraged. It is of so little use. But really, I would be lost without it. It is the only tool with which to do what must be done. In my mind that monkey wrench is of decisive importance. Possibly you feel like that monkey wrench, but if you could see yourself as God sees you, you would know that God needs you to do what could not be done without you. "Without God we cannot; without us God will not."

The Children of Israel thought they were God's "chosen people" and as such they ought to be superior. They did not understand that God had chosen them to serve mankind, to be the instrument of mankind's spiritual education. They were terribly important, but they failed to see why they were important. Without them God would not reveal Himself. They were not nobodies, even while they wandered in the desert. God needed them as He needs you and me. "How long will it be ere these people believe me?"

Like the Children of Israel, you will be pushed around by your ego and driven to behavior you will regret by the lure of

superiority, until you find your place as one of God's somebodies. It is important to notice, however, that on the road to
spiritual competence you will meet blank walls of frustration
that may well leave you exhausted physically and spiritually. So
we turn to the problem of personal frustration.

CHAPTER IV

Don't Fence Me In

THE popular song hit "Don't Fence Me In" is usually played or sung with the clippity-clop of horses' hoofs, and it conjures visions of limitless prairies and uninhibited movement. It gets under our skin with a bit of romantic nostalgia. Yesterday must have been wonderful! "Give a man a horse he could ride," and there were no fences to stop him. He could ride in any direction he pleased and be the master of his own fate. There was a world to conquer and a frontier for escape from home-town frustrations. Now we cannot run away. For better or for worse, we are fenced in, faced with the necessity of meeting our frustrations on the home range and finding meaning for our lives dealing creatively with obstacles.

The word "frustration" has come into vogue of late, not because it describes an experience that is new to our times, but because our generation has had an overdose of it. Actually the experience is as old as history. "Frustration" comes from the Latin *frustra,* and it means "in vain." It means to be thwarted by fences we cannot get through or over; to be blocked by circumstances beyond our control. It means wanting something we cannot have; striving for something that forever eludes us; reaching for something always beyond our grasp. Frustration is the experience of blundering into dead-end streets and blind alleys and getting nowhere for all our trying.

The more complicated our industrial society becomes, the more we are fenced in. In the slums of New York the Russian Jews, the South Italians, the Poles, and the Portuguese who work in the garment industries of the sweatshop era give voice to a common feeling when they sing:

> I work, work, work without end,
> Why and for whom I know not,
> I care not, I ask not.
> I am a machine.[1]

Everywhere there are men and women who have come to the unhappy conclusion that all roads lead nowhere. They have somewhat the feeling of Robert E. Lee when someone asked him the best way from Lexington, Virginia, to the outer world: "It makes little difference," said Lee, "for whichever route you select, you will wish you had taken the other."[2]

Times without number we have set off serenely on one road, only to wish we had taken some other. We meet frustration on every road. Again and again men have said in talking about their jobs: "There is no place to go. I'm stuck where I am for the rest of my life." Then there is the inevitable comment: "I should have made a change ten years ago." Two young people, dreaming lovely dreams, are married. They expect to be happy, but somehow they cannot seem to get along together. They feel fenced in, baffled. They wonder: "Maybe with Mary or Sue (or Bill or Jack) I could have been happy." But there is no room for second guessing. They cannot turn back. Everywhere there are people like the small boy who could not get along in school. Everything seemed to go wrong. Finally in desperation he said to his mother, "I try, and try, and try, but it doesn't do any good."

There are men and women who are fenced in, frustrated, by their physical limitations. They have weak hearts, rheumatism, aching backs, and migraine headaches. Every time they want to do something they have to say: "I can't. My heart won't let me." It is exasperating beyond measure. They plod through the days on the edge of disgust, now and then floundering into the abyss of despair. Why can't they be like other people? Why do they have to struggle against odds, with two strikes called on them before they start? They could accomplish something, be some-bodies, if they had their health!

Then there are those who are fenced in by responsibilities they cannot dodge. There are young men who cannot go to college because they have to help support their families. Weighted down by burdens they cannot escape, they live resent-ing the fates that made things so, trying not to be bitter and yet making a bad job of it. There are young women who want to get married, to build homes and have children, but they are needed at home. They are caught in the grip of circumstances they did not create. Their lives are fenced in and their hopes thwarted. They know the awful meaning of frustration.

You and I may as well face the blunt fact of frustration as one of life's inevitables. There is no escape from it, and sooner or later we are caught in its grip. The problem of life is to face frustration creatively, not to be deadened by it. It is important, therefore, to cancel out the reactions to frustration that are futile. Some roads lead us nowhere, and we are doomed if we choose them; other roads make frustration meaningful because they lead to power and wisdom.

There are three false roads through frustration that lead to personal failure and spiritual sterility, roads to be avoided like the plague. The first is the road of neurotic hostility. Dr. Jules Messerman of Northwestern University found that frustrated cats develop neurotic hostility very much as people do. He made the business of irritating cats into a fine art. He did not pull his cats' tails the way children do. That was too prosaic. He discovered that cats, like people, enjoy eating in peace and quiet. So Dr. Messerman made his cats neurotic with blasts of compressed air blown on their noses every time they reached for food. Some of the cats became spittingly and snarlingly aggressive. They took out their frustration on other cats. Normally peaceful, gentle cats became public enemies of cat society. They turned cat society into a bedlam of conflict. Just so, men frustrated in business turn their homes into armed camps of mutual hostility. Women frustrated at home upset church organizations and clubs. They are sources of endless irritation and unreasoned conflict. Children frustrated at home become problem children at school. People, like cats, are likely to become spittingly aggressive in their frustration. Unhappily, they only compound it.

The second road from frustration to futility is the road of defeatist helplessness. Again, cats are like people. Dr. Messerman discovered that some of his cats reacted to frustration with sheer "kittenish helplessness." Their frustration made them into defeatists. If they could not eat without annoying blasts of air, they simply would not eat. They would sit in corners and cry. They would whine piteously in their helpless defeat. They behaved like people who blunder into baffling circumstances and come away resigned to tearful despair. Such individuals are forever saying: "What's the use?" They fall, quite easily, into self-pity that laments: "Nobody loves me, everybody hates me."

The third road from frustration to futility is the road of escapism. No doubt Dr. Messerman's cats tried this road, but they were thoroughly fenced in. Meeting frustration, people try to run away. There are men who change jobs year after year. They move from one town to another trying to escape the frustration that follows them wherever they go. Thomas à Kempis is right, however: "Thou mayest change but not better thyself." As the old Dutch housewife in Edna Ferber's *So Big* tells the young teacher, "You can't run away from life, Missy; you can't run away far enough."[3] Nine times out of ten we run away from frustration only to run into more of the same.

Possibly we try to escape from frustration by means of drink or drugs. I never heard that frustration drove cats to drink, but experiments performed with mice at Marquette University[4] showed clearly that mice can be driven to drink. Students put two white mice, a male and a female, into a maze. Each was timed to see how long it would take to get from one end of the maze to a tray of grain at the other end. It took the male, named George, 220 seconds for the first trial. The female, named Myrtle, got there in 240 seconds.

After thirty such runs, the mice had speeded up considerably, Myrtle getting to the feedbox in forty-three seconds, George making it in fifty-nine seconds. Then the students played a mean trick on Myrtle. They put both mice in the maze, but they arranged it so that when Myrtle got to the goal George was already there nibbling on the grain. After innumerable runs, with George always getting to the grain well in advance of Myrtle, Myrtle began to get frustrated. She became nervous and excitable. And she turned to alcohol.

"At first," said Dr. Joachim LaMalta, psychologist in charge of the experiment, "neither of the mice cared for hard liquor. The boys put a couple of drops of the stuff into a dish of milk, and the mice refused to drink. But after Myrtle got neurotic, she began to take the milk again, with the alcohol. She's on her way to becoming an alcoholic, for the same reasons some humans become alcoholics—to relieve the outside strain and frustration."[5]

Of course, Myrtle did not speed up going through the maze when she became alcoholic. On the contrary, she slowed up so that on even terms she could not keep up with George. The more she drank, the more frustrated and neurotic she became.

So it is with humans. A young man in a contemporary novel described his father's plodding despair, and then how his father would go on periodic sprees. He would spend money he did not have and get gloriously drunk. By way of explanation the young man remarked: "It was dad's way of spitting in fate's eye." Most of us would like to pay our respects to fate now and then, just to relieve our pent-up frustrations and to escape from the burden of defeat. Nevertheless, "spitting in fate's eye" by indulging in a spree is a sure way of landing in futility.

There are multitudes of defeated men and women who have met their frustrations foolishly, like cats or mice. They are beset by neurotic hostility, defeatism, escapism, or they are candidates for Skid Row. They live without luster; they struggle without any sense of significance; they plod without power; and they die without regret. They have come to the devastating conclusion that all roads lead nowhere. Nothing, they are sure, can change anything.

The most obvious and yet the most deceptive fact about frustration is that it is the consequence of circumstances beyond our control. We were born into a particular environment that determined the way of our going. We were bequeathed certain hereditary weaknesses, and we had nothing to do with our heredity or our environment. The economic forces that thwart our goals often are beyond our control. Our physical limitations frequently are not our fault. We were born with a certain mental capacity, beyond the limits of which we cannot go. We are fenced in by circumstances we did not create and cannot seem to change. Nevertheless, paradoxical as it may seem, the key to the conquest of frustrating circumstances is "not in our stars but in ourselves." An obstacle is not merely an obstacle. Every obstacle in life's way involves a personal equation. A fence is a fence to a cow, but to a deer a fence is merely an excuse for a high jump. A sand trap on a golf course is an impossible hazard for a novice, but it presents no problem to an expert.

Obviously, it does no good to wish we were what we are not. The fenced-in cow would be a fool to grow neurotic because she is not a deer. A cow is a cow and you are you. You have capacities and powers, and you ought to stretch them to the limit, but you need the wit to see the difference between the possible and the impossible. Sometimes we are like children crying for the moon, wanting what we cannot have. There is the man whose voice does very nicely in a barbershop quartet, but he wants to sing grand opera. Innumerable frustrated people are like the little girl who said to her mother: "When I grow up I'm going to be a father!" The ambition was altogether beyond the bounds of the possible. If you are a brunette, there is no use wishing you had red hair. If you are short, there is no use being frustrated because you are not tall.

The first step toward the conquest of frustration is, therefore, a degree of realism and the honesty to face facts. There are some things you cannot be or do no matter how desperately you try. Quite possibly you cannot be a beauty queen. In all probability you are not a genius. Society being what it is, maybe you never can move in "the best" social circles. There is no use making yourself miserable because some roads are blocked and cannot be cut through. A football player put the truth with wisdom when he remarked: "I did not really find myself until I gave up trying to be a star." Clearly, there are some frustrations that have to be conquered by way of surrender. If we cannot have the moon, quite possibly we can do very well without it. If we cannot be world-beaters, we still can be useful citizens. We cultivate not a little misery for ourselves and an unnecessary burden of frustration by wanting the impossible.

Most of us, Horatio Alger to the contrary notwithstanding, cannot be presidents or captains of industry. We may as well face the fact of our own limitations. One woman noted discerningly, "The happiest day of my life was the day I gave up trying to be beautiful." One of the noblest men I know long since gave up trying to be a bank president and settled down to be the best bank teller in town. When he finally came to terms with his own limitations and began to make the most of his assets in a job for which he was admirably fitted, he ceased to be upset and irritated when promotions went to other men.

Sooner or later we are constrained to accept ourselves and to comprehend both our limitations and our capacities. We need what Leon Saul calls "a grasp of reality." Often it is our false images of ourselves that lead us to frustration and misery. We pretend we are any man's equal if only we could persuade others to see us as we see ourselves. Willie, who marches through life to a tragic end in *The Death of a Salesman,* is an exaggerated illustration of human pretense. Willie was a magnificent pretender. He was very ordinary, really, but he pushed through life acting like a king. He made it clear to his two sons that he was a somebody. He knew the right people. He had contacts. He was a world-beater, a super-go-getter. He could get a job anywhere, and he stayed with his mediocre job with the old firm just because he was loyal. Really the firm could not get along without him. But it was all a false image, a shell of pretense that had to be punctured. It was punctured with a sickening pop when the old firm decided Willie was not needed.

Willie coveted the influence, position, recognition of other men, and when he could not get what he wanted, he pretended he had it and lived a masquerade of deception. If he had spent half as much time really making the most of himself as he spent pretending to be a howling success, he could have been respected and honored. At least he could have respected himself and given his sons a father they could respect. As it was, he blundered through life in perpetual frustration. In the end, he lost everything, just pretending.

Paul understood the peril of pretending, of holding false images, when he wrote: "Let no man think of himself more highly than he ought to think."[6] The admonition is both psychologically and spiritually sound. Those who think too highly of themselves are inescapably frustrated. No one else will accept their self-estimate because it is essentially false. An inflated ego is an invitation to frustration. Don't sell yourself short; but don't oversell yourself either. Make the most of what there is in you and then accept yourself and come to terms with your limitations.

Always it is important to recognize the difference between outward obstacles that can be overcome by inner discipline, courage, and faith, and personal limitations of mind and capacity that must be accepted. You may be fitted to be a first-class plumber at the same time you are fitted to be a complete failure as a preacher, or vice versa. The story of the young man who went to a theological seminary saying he had had a vision that compelled him to be a preacher is suggestive. He said he had seen two great letters etched in the clouds: "P.C." He said he knew God was calling him to "Preach Christ." After examining the lad's credentials and observing his I.Q. the seminary dean remarked, "Son, I am inclined to think the letters in the sky really meant 'Plow corn.'"

Actually, of course, preaching and plowing both are high callings of God, and a man can be decisively useful and creative either behind a plow or in a pulpit. If a man can plow a straight furrow and raise a worthy crop there is no use in his feeling frustrated because he cannot preach. The expert electrician would be foolish to feel frustrated because he does not have the capacity to be an industrial magnate. There are some obstacles you can overcome and some you cannot. Frustration is the consequence of not recognizing the difference between the two. It is a legacy bequeathed to those who refuse to accept themselves.

Just as it is essential to accept the facts about ourselves, it also is important to accept the facts about other people. More often than not our frustrations involve others who win the prizes we want, do what we cannot do, and seem to have all the advantages. We may as well accept the fact that nature created us unequal. There are others who have capacities and powers we lack. So, if you want to be frustrated and miserable, just look at yourself beside somebody with five talents to match against your one. He has a mind that sweeps grandly through small details to the main issue. He has endless endurance, never seems to be tired. You have a mind that has to struggle with minor details and seldom escapes from them. You have a small store of physical stamina and hardly know what it means to be anything but weary. He has a personality that makes him the center of the table no matter where he sits. You are drab and colorless. He can wear a lumberman's shirt and no tie and look like a prince. You can dress up in a stiff shirt and tails and look mine run. You can work yourself into a state of frustrated emotional turbulence resenting what he has that you haven't.

Sooner or later, if you wish to conquer your sense of frustration, you will accept your neighbor and learn to love him and to rejoice in his gifts. A high-school student I know had his heart set on being president of the student body. He almost made it, but not quite. Another young man with great gifts of mind and personality won the coveted post. It was some time before the defeated candidate could accept the lad who had defeated him. He moped and he was resentful. Frustration weighed heavily upon him. Finally he went to his minister, who suggested he might make a real friend of the boy who had beaten him. Then he might feel better. He agreed to try.

Months passed, and out of the experiment came a rich and rewarding friendship. But more important was the fact that the defeated young man escaped his sense of frustration. He supported, encouraged, and helped the student body president. He even rejoiced in the triumphs of his friend, and in so doing won a glorious victory for himself. If you can "rejoice with them that rejoice" in their victories you have won life's noblest triumph. If you can feel a sense of satisfaction when your neighbor climbs higher, goes farther, and achieves more than you can match, you have achieved maturity and taken a long and important step toward creative self-management.

The words "love thine enemy" are the essence of wisdom. The enemy who thwarts your goals, gets what you want, always seems to be ahead of you, is a major source of frustration until you learn to love him and to rejoice with him in his triumphs. Your frustration is mostly a consequence of your egocentric predicament, an indication of the fact that you have not yet shifted the center of your existence from yourself to others. Freedom lies in the will to love even thine enemy.

If we are to manage our frustrations we necessarily begin by accepting ourselves and we follow through by accepting others. The third step is to recognize that the key to conquest of most outward obstacles is basically within us. Before we are able to deal with our frustrations it is imperative that we deal with ourselves. All roads lead nowhere if we ride off in all directions with irritated indignation when we blunder into fences that hem us in. We get nowhere with neurotic hostility, defeatism, or escapism, but "in quietness and confidence" we often can find ways through or around or over the fences that thwart us.

Biography testifies to the power of the spirit to overcome thwarting fences. Demosthenes, the stutterer, orating to the roaring sea with his mouth full of pebbles, won his way to clarity of speech and eloquence. Henry Ward Beecher, a "clumsy, bashful boy, his speech blurred by an enlarged palate," took himself in hand and pushed on to poise and power. Thomas Edison blundered into one obstacle after another on his way to the secret of the electric light. Cloyd M. Chapman describes how he found Edison one night in his laboratory, his face wreathed in smiles. Thinking Edison had solved the problem of the incandescent light, he was astonished when Edison remarked, "Not a blamed thing works. Now I can start over." Notice the words "Now I can start over." They suggest the inner spirit that carried him over the obstacles in his path.

When Robert Louis Stevenson became an invalid it seemed as if the doors to the future had closed upon him. He could have floundered into despair. See him propped up in bed, wincing now and then with pain. But there was an inner spirit whose ministry refused to admit the finality of frustration, and one visiting Stevenson might have seen him surrounded by pillows but playing cheerful tunes on his flute, or busy, despite pain, writing the stories you and I have come to know and to love. The conquest of frustration had nothing to do with the change of outward circumstances. It was altogether an affair of the spirit.

When we have faced the fact that the problem of meeting frustration is inward, it is reasonably clear that thinking is more useful than fretting. Give your mind a chance to take command of your emotions. Quite possibly you can think your way through your frustration, but when you do your thinking with your feelings and let your moods overwhelm your mind, you are like the music that goes round and round without ever coming to a conclusion. Thinking balances positives and negatives in frustrating situations and quietly looks for a way out. It asks honest questions. Is it possible to go over the obstacles with courage and persistence? Am I crying for the moon? Is it possible to find a detour that will bring fulfillment to life along a new road? These questions are fundamental. They are questions of the mind and not the heart.

No man ever found more frustrating circumstances than George Washington Carver, the eminent Negro scientist. The first requirement of a scientist is a laboratory, but Tuskegee Institute, where Professor Carver labored, had no laboratory and no money for equipment. When he wanted a simple thing like sandpaper, he could not buy it. Once, when he was fretting over what to do about sandpaper, he lay down and fell asleep. In his dream he walked into a wagon shop. He went up to a man putting a tire on a wagon wheel and asked the man if he knew how to make sandpaper. "Yes," replied the man, but he failed to enlighten the questioner. Finally, Professor Carver said: "I'll tell you how to do it." And he described a process he thought might be correct. "You did it all right," the man said, "except you did not boil the sand." Professor Carver awakened, went to his laboratory, boiled the sand, and the sandpaper was as it should be.

Of course, Professor Carver had been thinking, wrestling with the problem of sandpaper and how to make it. The dream was but the subconscious mind carrying on the thinking of consciousness. "There's no use to whine, 'Oh, if I only had so-and-so,' " he used to tell his students. "Do it anyhow; use what you find about you." Then he would go with them to junk heaps for bottles, jars, and wires to make what they could not buy. "Equipment is not all in the laboratory, but partly in the head of the man running it."[7]

In the Old Testament there are two word portraits of Elijah that suggest the futility of emotion and the sanity of reason in dealing with frustration. Etched in vivid words is the picture of Elijah in an emotional tailspin weeping beneath a juniper tree. The struggle against Queen Jezebel and her priests seemed lost. There was no hope, and Elijah was a picture of lonely despair. He had come apart at the seams. He was frayed out and all to pieces. He saw no possibilities in his situation, nothing but blank and irretrievable defeat. The world was against him and nobody was on his side.

The second portrait is painted atop Mount Horeb, where

Elijah fled to get away from it all. He had been asleep, listening in his dreams to the roar of earthquake, wind, and fire, grim reminders of the struggle with Jezebel. Rubbing his eyes, Elijah was startled by the voice of God asking a very embarrassing question: "What are you doing here, Elijah?"[8] Elijah might have answered that he was trying to get his emotions under control so that he could think things through, but he had not thought of that. Instead he explained his heroic struggle and pointed to the fact that he was hemmed in now and afraid. "They seek my life, to take it away," he complained. Quite literally God said to Elijah: "You have let your emotions run away with your mind. Your trouble is you. You are not alone; there are seven thousand others in Israel who are on your side, and I, the Lord God of Israel, am on your side, too." When he stopped to think, Elijah discovered some very positive factors at work on his side. When he let his mind go to work on his problem, he took the shortest road back where he belonged and carried on to a triumph he might have lost.

Our experience is very much like Elijah's. We are utterly helpless and undone until our minds take charge of our emotions and we take ourselves in hand. There are parents, for example, baffled and frustrated by the impossible behavior of a son or a daughter. One thing is clear: They will not be able to manage their child until their minds take command of their emotions and they get themselves in hand. Here is a man whose business is not doing too well. He has a nervous stomach and high blood pressure because, he says, of business burdens. Pardon me if I say that is nonsense. He has a nervous stomach and high blood pressure because his nerves and emotions are running riot. He has not taken command of himself. He is not running his business; he is being run by it. His tension is unbearable, and he cannot control his business until his mind controls his emotions.

When we begin to think in the presence of our frustrations we are confronted by the blunt fact of human experience that when one road is blocked, nine times out of ten there is another road open. Fenced in in one direction, we find possibilities of value in some other direction. Detours may be annoying, but they can lead to fulfillment if we do not give up without trying to find a way through. Says Arnold Bennett:

A man may desire to go to Mecca. His conscience tells him he ought to go to Mecca. He fares forth, either by the aid of Cook's or unassisted. He may never reach Mecca. He may drown before he gets to Port Said; he may perish ingloriously on the coast of the Red Sea; his desire may remain eternally frustrated. Unfulfilled aspirations always trouble him. But he will not be tormented in the same way as the man who, desiring to reach Mecca, and harried by the desire to reach Mecca, never leaves Brixton. It is something to have left Brixton. Most of us have not left Brixton. We have not even taken a cab to Ludgate Circus.[9]

So, when one road is blocked, we can sit and mourn or we can set out for Mecca on another road. That is far better than just sitting still.

I remember an eighty-three-year-old lady whose funeral service I once conducted. She never had married because she had her mother to take care of for many years. She wanted a home and children, but she was thoroughly fenced in. She might have become an embittered spinster, defeated by circumstances. With one road blocked, she took another. If she could not have a home and children of her own, still she could give her life to children. She became a kindergarten teacher and then organized a school for kindergarten teachers. She was radiant through the years. She loved life. When she was dying, she chuckled through her pain and remarked: "Funny, but I don't know how to die. I never did it before." Her frustration was by no means final; she found a detour around it.

Timothy Dwight, one-time president of Yale University,

looked back upon the failure of his eyes as a kind event within God's providence. The permanent weakness of his eyes altered his habits. It closed the road to scholarship and left his plans frustrated. But, he discovered, if he could not read, he could meditate. He could not study as he wished, but he could observe. He could not go on mastering the classics of the world by firsthand research, but he could extract information from conversation. Years after the failure of his eyes he noted that the most useful information comes, not from reading books, but from reading life itself. Ruined eyes did not keep him from being a great teacher and from learning what he wanted to know. He found a new road through the fence that thwarted his intention. He echoed the observation of the *Blind Plowman,* "God took away my sight that my soul might see."

Again and again men and women have been thwarted on one road only to find another road to triumph. Pasteur dreamed of being a soldier, fighting for the glory of France, but his crippled body frustrated that dream; the thwarted soldier turned into a genius. Loyola, wounded, his military career ended, turned into a saint who left the world richer for his having lived in it. Charles Darwin floundered into failure as a medical student and then detoured around the frustration to triumph as a naturalist. Let it be remembered that, for every road that is closed, another is open!

When we meet obstacles that thwart our progress it is important to recognize that sometimes obstacles are opportunities in disguise. If, as Thoreau says, most men live lives of "quiet desperation," it is because they see no possibilities in their frustrations. They simply accept the fact they have come to a dead-end street, and that's that. Happily there are others who find themselves fenced in by circumstances and who promptly begin to explore the possibilities. When mosquitoes, bearing yellow fever, prevented the building of the Panama Canal, there were those who looked on the enterprise as finished. Others, however, recognized an opportunity. To them yellow fever was a challenge, something to be conquered. Panama was an opportunity to discover the secret of yellow fever and put an end to it.

Sometimes in life we take the path of least resistance until we blunder into frustrations that make us take a fresh look at the road we are traveling. A man I know spent half of his life as a mediocre accountant. Then the company that employed him was sold and he found himself out of a job. It seemed like a tragedy until he remembered he had always wanted to be a salesman but never had the nerve to give up his job and try it. Actually, his frustration turned out to be a great opportunity and he is happier and better off than he ever would have been as an accountant.

Or take the experience of Nathaniel Hawthorne. When he was eliminated from his post in the Salem Customs House by a trick of village politics, his world tumbled in. He had the wit to see, however, that his frustration could be creative. He wrote to his friend George S. Hillard, "Under God's guidance I shall arrive at something better." His capable and loyal wife faced the loss of her husband's job with the remark: "Oh, then you can write your book." The book was *The Scarlet Letter*. Hawthorne's frustration in one direction turned out to be an open road in another. His obstacle was his opportunity.

Thus the experiences of frustration that seem to be caused by outward circumstances can be met creatively. One man's obstacle is another man's opportunity. One man's dead-end street is another's invitation to inventiveness. Arnold Toynbee notes that in history the challenge of frustrating circumstances has been the impetus of progress. Crushing outward conditions have inspired conquering inward courage. Time and again men and women have turned obstacles into opportunities, frustrations into open doors to a larger future.

The upshot of the matter is that our frustrations can be a means of growth. Certainly it is true that character is the consequence of dealing creatively with what we cannot avoid. We cannot avoid obstacles, but we can turn them into tools by which to fashion our souls. Gina Kaus remarks that Catherine the Great "flourished in adversity" and "grew great by her capacity for enduring humiliation." Her husband was a disreputable man, who flaunted his mistress before his wife and the whole court. But, by way of her humiliation, Catherine won the greatest struggle of her career—she won self-mastery and inner serenity. Catherine's obstacle was not an easy one to conquer, but her humiliation, her frustration as a wife, turned out to be the anvil on which she shaped her character.

Frustration is neutral in itself. A homely face, for example, can be extremely frustrating. It can make a woman bitter, resentful, and more homely and unattractive than she need be. On the other hand, a homely face can be a stimulus to inner beauty and radiant personality. If the beauty parlor won't help, something inside will. Some of the most attractive women I know would waste their time entering a beauty contest, but they have an ineffable something on the inside that makes them beautiful. They have cultivated the inner resources that many of their prettier contemporaries have neglected.

If our frustrations make us dig for compensating values they are sources of inner growth. I know a preacher, for example, who has a voice like an old saw. He knows it, but he has overcome the frustration of it. He has done everything possible to improve his voice, but it remains anything but musical. Nature simply skimped on his vocal chords. Nevertheless, he is a great preacher. He uses a poor instrument to say vital things. He has compensated for a poor voice with magnificent thought and spiritual insight. After the first three minutes of a sermon nobody notices his voice because he has something decisive to say. He has turned the frustration of a miserable voice into a stimulus to vital thinking.

Some time ago a preacher friend of mine told me the story of a one-legged rooster that belongs to a farmer he knows. The farmer keeps the rooster so that he will be reminded that obstacles and frustrating handicaps need not be fatal. The rooster gets around the farmyard on one leg faster than any hen in the place. He sleeps on one leg, eats standing on one leg, and he has even developed a technique of scratching with his toes. What is more, he can crow. In fact, the farmer insists his one-legged friend can outcrow any rooster in the country. There are times in the early morning when the rooster seems to be proclaiming his conquest of frustration and compensating for the limitation of one leg with a powerful voice.

The obvious truth is that when we are fenced in by obstacles and difficulties of one sort or another we surrender or we grow, one or the other; we give up or we move in new directions with expanded capacities. Either we meet our frustrations understanding that they hide possibilities of growth under their rough exterior or we collapse into plaintiveness and despair. The only real tragedy of being fenced in is bitterness, resentment over the fact that obstacles block our way. If you are fenced in by the inadequacy of your formal education, it is enervating to sit back complaining resentfully that you did not have a chance. If you are frustrated by the fact that you have a mediocre mind, it is tragic to assume you were treated unfairly when God distributed His gifts. You really were not cheated. On the contrary, there are compensating gifts in you that you were meant to discover and use. Your apparent frustrations may well turn out to be decisive advantages that challenge you to grow.

Certainly there are times when obstacles stab sleeping powers awake. There is a hint of the truth in Opal Leigh Berryman's delightful biography of her father, *Pioneer Preacher*. She tells the story of her father's visit with Sheriff Lubeck, who had been pursuing a thief. One by one the clues had vanished until the sheriff was left with nothing but his determination to find the man he sought. When the sheriff departed after a fruitless questioning of the preacher, Opal said to her father: "Why doesn't he give up?" "Sometimes," her father replied, "obstacles wear spurs."[10] So they may, but whether or not "obstacles wear spurs" depends upon what the obstacles find in those they confront. Obstacles may also wear a shroud.

In the final summing up, whether obstacles wear spurs or a shroud depends upon whether they drive us to God or to despair. Whether the fact that we are fenced in becomes an advantage or a disadvantage depends upon whether it creates in us a feeling of unfair limitation or a sense of spiritual need. One advantage of an experience of frustration lies in the fact that it may inspire a sense of need for resources beyond ourselves. It was so in the experience of St. Paul, for in writing to the Ephesians he noted that in the moments of his greatest need he found "a mighty increase of strength by his Spirit in the inner man."[11]

In ordinary life two experiences call out the consciousness of spiritual need: being up against something too much for us and undertaking something too hard for us. There are people who labor under the burden of frustration much of the time. Their "reach is beyond their grasp." At every turn of the road they are reminded of their limitations. At the moment they wish to adventure greatly, but they are fenced in by their responsibilities. The loads they are required to carry are heavier than they should be asked to bear. Again and again they are confronted by the fact that their obvious resources are inadequate to see them through. But, whether they know it or not, they are on the threshold of "a mighty increase of strength by his Spirit in the inner man." Their sense of need, their awareness of their own inadequacy, is the opening wedge to spiritual power. As Dr. Moffatt translates the first Beatitude, "Blessed are they who feel their spiritual need; for theirs is the kingdom of heaven."

Certainly the early Christians were over their heads when they set out to win the world. They were an unimpressive lot, fenced in on every hand. The disciples were "ignorant and unlearned men," at a severe disadvantage as they went about the task of creating the Christian fellowship. Nevertheless, their frustrations made them aware of their spiritual need, and they found inner resources to see them through. Most of those who followed Jesus were at a disadvantage in their pagan world. Many of them were poor, sick, lame, blind, or mentally disturbed. But they were aware of their spiritual need, and in Jesus they found "a mighty increase of strength." Within the first three centuries the fenced-in Christians flung their faith around the world. They "upset the world."

Obstacles in our path are potential instruments of spiritual growth and power. Frustrations may drive us to neurotic hostility, defeatism, or escapism—or they may lead us to God. But if our frustrations lead us to God we discover Paul was right when he noted that "in him who strengtheneth me, I am able for anything." Without God, our frustrations manage us; with Him, we can manage our frustrations. As Henry Drummond noted after talking with innumerable frustrated, troubled men and women, "Peace is the possession of adequate reserves."

Certainly our adequacy to manage ourselves when we are fenced in depends upon the possession of spiritual reserves. "Thou dost keep him in perfect peace whose mind is stayed on thee."[12] Those words came from Isaiah the prophet, and they did not come from an ivory tower. They sprang from a stormy time when Israel was threatened with disaster and the exile was just around the corner. They were spoken just a little while before Sennacherib and the Assyrians laid siege to Jerusalem. They were uttered when men and women were afraid they could not manage the stress of their times. But Isaiah knew they never could handle their troubles without spiritual reserves to hold them steady.

When I was a boy I used to play in a little stream that ran in front of our mountain cottage. I can remember trying to dam that little stream with rocks and mud. At first it was easy, but the little stream always defeated me in the end by bringing never-ending reserves from the rear. First the water would break out to the left, and when I stopped it there, it would break out on the right. Blocked in one direction it forced its way through in another until my dam collapsed. Jesus would have us understand that life with God is like that little stream. It cannot be stopped because there are endless reserves to keep it going.

Jesus never would have meant what he means to the world if he had not managed himself so magnificently in the face of his frustrations. His enemies hemmed him in on all sides. They tried to undermine him with lies and false accusations. They threatened him, put obstacles in his way, and at last crowned him with thorns and crucified him between two thieves. Why did he conquer? Why did his cross of shame become a symbol of triumph? The early Christians had the answer: "God was in Christ," and even death could not stop him. He had endless reserves to see him through his frustration. All through the centuries he has been trying to tell us that God can be in us, too. He has been trying to tell us there are new inward gates in the old outward fences that hem us in.

CHAPTER V

Released from Tension

W HY don't you relax?" I asked a man who had come to my office in a state of nervous tension. He looked at me with obvious irritation and replied: "My God, I wish I knew how." While we sat and talked he smoked one cigarette after another. He fidgeted in his chair and nervously rubbed his face. Obviously he was wound up like a spring. He had to be "on his toes," he said, to manage his business and make a profit. "With competition the way it is," he observed, "nobody can let down at all." Everything about the man suggested that he felt pushed, crowded, under pressure. He was close to the breaking point and he knew it.

The man in my office was but one of the innumerable nervous casualties of our "step-lively-don't-block-traffic" civilization. Our "get results" culture, symbolized by an army of "go-getter" salesmen, has left us nervously, physically, and spiritually exhausted. The heroes of our culture are the active and the animated. We think there is something lacking in the man who has "time on his hands." If we are not really "very busy," we pretend to be so on the assumption that busy-ness is a primary virtue. In order to be in tune with our times we have to be going somewhere—anywhere—under a full head of steam.

To be sure, there are times when we need to drive, to get things done under pressure, but under the impetus of our "get-things-done" way of life our keyed-up mood has become a habit, and an exhausting one at that. We wear ourselves down going places whether we need to go or not. We join this and that just to keep busy because we don't know what to do with ourselves when we stop. We dread the solitude of our own company and retreat from aloneness into the refuge of activity. So we have neither time nor inclination to cultivate the friendship of great books or to grapple with the great issues of life and death. Living under tension our lives have few anchors in deep conviction or stabilizing belief.

It would be folly to deny that there is a place for tension in our lives, for drive and pressure. Frequently we create under the pressure of necessity. There is, for example, the creative tension of the public speaker, keyed up for a dynamic address, or the tension of a businessman, stretching his mind to embrace all the factors involved in a difficult decision. There is the tension of a salesman, trying to keep one jump ahead of his customer's sales resistance. The athlete, ready for a supreme effort, has to reach a fine point of creative tension in order to function at his best. Many an upset on the gridiron has come about because one team or the other played "over its head."

The human mind creates under pressure. Often we do our best work when we are driven by necessity. Our powers are focused in a great concentration. We think with clarity and produce with facility. It took the terrible tension of a crisis to inspire the genius of Winston Churchill, and the crowding pressure of circumstances to make Oliver Cromwell what he was. Arnold Toynbee noted in *A Study of History* that the unrelenting pressure of necessity stirs the creative powers of men and brings out the greatness that is in them.

It is important to notice, however, that tension, to be meaningful and creative, has to be temporary. Even a rubber band that is perpetually stretched loses its resilience. To be constantly keyed up, on the move, pressing, is to cultivate destructive tension. If we never let go we arrive at the point where we are unable to hang on. A businessman put the matter pointedly when he observed: "I've come to the point where I can't keep going and I can't stop." A mother, feeling the pressure of raising four children, phrased her feeling with the remark: "I'm living for that blessed day when all my children are grown and married." Then, as an afterthought, she added, "I hope I can last that long."

Mechanical engineers, studying the strength of metals, know that every metal has a "fatigue limit." Take a piece of stiff wire, for example, and flex it repeatedly and vigorously. Nothing may happen for perhaps one hundred bendings. Then, the one hundred and first time it is bent, the wire may snap, as if it had suddenly become as brittle as a dry twig. So in designing automobiles or freight cars the engineers take account of the "fatigue limit" of every moving or vibrating part. They are aware that under the constant stress of use there is a limit to the resilience of even the strongest metals.

There is also a personality "fatigue limit"—a point at which personality goes to pieces and we lose our capacity for self-management and self-control. When tension is a normal condition hour after hour, the least added pressure brings us to the "fatigue limit." When you are hurrying to prepare dinner for your family after a busy and trying day without relief from tension, the extra pressures are too much. When the telephone rings and the doorbell rings, the dog barks, the soup boils over, and one of the children yells, "Mom," all at the same time, it is just too much to bear. It is not the work that bothers you; it is the accumulated tension of the day plus the extra demand for which you are not prepared. By the time you sit down to the dinner table your appetite is gone and your enthusiasm for life is at low ebb. In all likelihood your husband comes home from work in a similar state of nervous tension. He reminds you pointedly that he is "tuckered." That is his subtle way of telling you he is not going to set the table if he can help it. He was under strain all day at the office, and the rush hour traffic coming home was no picnic. At that point, it takes something more than phenobarbital to keep your nerves manageable.

Modern life is demanding. The pace is terrific. Like the Red Queen in *Alice in Wonderland,* we have to run furiously just to stand still, much less get ahead. So we gear our lives to a fast trot and get into the habit of trotting all the time. We hurry to bed and we hurry to get up. No wonder we cannot sleep. The druggists make a neat profit from our insomnia, and sleeping pills have become a million-dollar business. Within us there is the fury of endless agitation and tension. Even our children do not escape the strain of tension. One small boy came home from a busy day at school, followed by a music lesson and a class at the Y.M.C.A., threw himself into a chair, and remarked: "Mom, I've been hurrying all day and I don't know why."

Unhappily, hurrying through the days under tension the way we do, we make foolish mistakes, as I did not long ago coming home from Chicago after a day of hurrying. I rushed down the steps to the subway reaching the platform just as a train was about to pull out. I hopped through a door as it was closing and the train started. But something seemed wrong. I turned to a man standing beside me and asked: "Which way am I going, north or south?" He smiled and answered: "I don't know which way you wanted to go, but you are going south." Sheepishly I got off at the next station and took another train going north.

Time and again under the pressure of our days we go the

wrong way when even a moment's thought would save us. We make wrong decisions, false judgments, and stupid mistakes while we are victims of the hurry habit that infects our times. Our mistakes generate irritation and increase tension. In the long run we lose time by hurrying and we accumulate a motley collection of tensions that lead us to and beyond our "fatigue limit."

Obviously, we cannot change the tempo, the furious pace of the world around us. We cannot go back to the slow-moving world of Grey's "Elegy" in which

> The curfew tolls the knell of parting day,
> The lowing herd wind slowly o'er the lea,
> The plowman homeward plods his weary way,
> And leaves the world to darkness and to me.[1]

In our world, neon lights blot out the darkness and the stars and Spike Jones or Bing Crosby takes over the silence that once belonged to me.

If we are to find inner peace and poised relaxation we shall have to find it in spite of the world and in the midst of tension. It will have to be an affair of the spirit wrought by stern self-discipline. At the outset, we shall have to take an honest look at our lives and our activities. As a wise physician said to a young woman busy with raising three children: "You will have to judge what you undertake in the light of the question: Will it make any difference six months from now?" That question is important for all of us. When we find ourselves nervous, tense, and unable to stop, it is time for us to look at the things we are doing and to ask ourselves whether they will mean anything six months from now.

Sometimes I have a gnawing suspicion that half of our activities simply drain our energies, leaving us poorer, not richer. They leave us no wiser and no better than we were and they add nothing to the wealth of the world. They merely help us to "kill time" while creating the illusion that we are very busy and very important. One sensitive woman put the truth wisely when she remarked: "I've been so busy running from club to club, from canasta to bridge, from luncheon to tea that I haven't had time to do one thing that mattered. Beginning now I am reorganizing my life."

What is true of women is true also of men. A friend who had a heart attack and of necessity reorganized his life observed sadly: "During the two months I spent in bed I had plenty of time to think and I know now that hurried business trips I thought were necessary were not necessary. Banquets and dinners and luncheons I thought were essential were unessential. It almost cost me my life to get wise." Quite possibly it will cost you your life if you do not "get wise." You cannot live under the strain of perpetual tension without paying a price.

Take time to plan your days. Ask yourself whether you are spending your energy profitably, or just spending it. I remember listening once to an efficiency expert who had made an analysis of how salesmen spend their time. According to the expert, there were those who hurried from customer to customer, furiously rushing hither and yon, burning energy by the barrel, and producing little for all their fury. There were others who planned their days carefully, taking time to analyze the needs of their customers, to prepare attractive and pertinent sample displays, and thinking through their approach to each customer problem. They gave the impression of efficient leisure, of knowing precisely where they were going and why. They put far more real work into less time than their hurrying competitors did. They used their enforced waiting time for thinking, not fretting; for planning, not fuming. They did not seem half as busy as those who were furiously bouncing from customer to customer, but they were far more productive. They planned their days with an eye upon six months or a year hence, building good will, confidence, and friendship, creating lasting values while they moved thoughtfully from customer to customer.

It is not planned living but frittered living that creates tension. It is flying off in all directions at once and going nowhere that leaves us exhausted, weighted down with a sense of futility. So, if you are tense, nervous, and fatigued, take a long look at your life. Ask yourself how much of what you are doing will matter six months from now. Start today planning for tomorrow so as to eliminate unnecessary strain.

There is another simple and yet important antidote for tension. Our children call it play. Never get too old or too important to play. After a funeral service for a man of fifty-five, his widow remarked: "Jim was all business; he never learned to play." No doubt Jim was secretly proud of the fact that he was all business. Probably he felt he was too big, too important to play. However, the concern for which he worked seems to be carrying on very nicely without Jim. The business did not cave in after Jim was buried. No doubt Jim's pride is a bit deflated in his heaven for tired businessmen. While he was here he would not believe he was expendable!

Golf may be the answer to the need for play for some men. On the other hand, there are those who simply do not play at playing golf. A preacher friend of mine plays golf on the run. At the end of nine holes he is exhausted, irritated, and tense. He works at playing, and golf leaves him with his tension unrelieved. Too many men are like that. They play golf under pressure. When they slice or hook or miss an easy shot they get all tied up in knots of exasperation. They might as well have gone on working.

Some men play at their hobbies. I know a man who finds his fun in fishing. On long winter nights he makes flies and plugs. Call on him at his home, and he will get out his fishing equipment, fondle it lovingly, and tell you which plug took his biggest bass. Every plug brings back a story of some visit to a near-by lake, and his memory recaptures the fine details of a day's fishing. Under the spell of his tackle box, business is blotted out, problems are forgotten, and life is sheer joy. Tension and pressure evaporate for him as he lays the wings on a ginger quill and imaginatively drops it into the riffles of his favorite trout stream.

There are men who play in their gardens, finding freedom from tension in cultivating roses, turning back yards into places of beauty and refreshment. The cares and concerns of the day vanish when they don old clothes and put their hands into the good earth. Turning over the soil with a strong fork is not work; it is play. Planting a new type of rose bush is an adventure. Each new bud is greeted with eagerness and curiosity and the flowering is a major triumph. The garden, rich with the mystery of growing things, is a means to creative play and an escape from tension.

Creative play, a hobby of one sort or another will do more for you than synthetic play. Television, the theater, the movies have a place, but they are likely to leave you where they found you. It is better to sing "Sweet Adeline" off key yourself than to listen to a prize barbershop quartet on the radio. It is better to walk a mile for exercise than to sit in a stuffy arena watching a prize fight. It is better by far to ride a horse than to watch Roy Rogers pounding across the plains on Trigger. Real play requires something of you and gives something to you. Play at its best takes all there is of you, body, mind, and spirit, and it leaves you free from tension.

Needless to say, you need a reasonable amount of rest. Paradoxically, tension creates fatigue and fatigue creates tension. The two walk hand in hand. I know a busy woman who has learned to sleep ten minutes twice a day. How she does it is beyond me, but her cat naps mark the difference between tension and fatigue and a fine quality of tireless but relaxed energy. She says her naps are the secret of poise. Knowing her, I am inclined to think she is right.

You may find it quite impossible to take two ten-minute naps a day, or even one, but you can organize your life so that you get enough sleep. Maybe you can manage one night a week staying out until the wee small hours, but you cannot manage a steady diet of night life without blundering into tension and fatigue. Common sense suggests that when entertaining and being entertained get to the point of creating weariness and taut nerves, they are not worth what they cost. Not even business, carried home in your brief case, is worth what it costs if it robs you of your rest and brings you to the point of nervous exhaustion. Sleep heals many things, "winding up the raveled sleeve of care." The man who conserves his energies with reasonable rest can accomplish prodigious amounts of work without exhaustion. Fatigue, on the other hand, makes even play quite impossible. Without adequate rest, play becomes work, and life turns into an endless struggle without relief.

Plan and rest and play! These are three necessary ingredients in any life that has learned to manage tension. It should be added, then: take time to think, to separate the sheep from the goats in your experience. Learn to ignore the insignificant and concentrate on the vital. There is a bit of priceless wisdom in the philosophy of Joe Page of the New York Yankees, who in 1949 established his reputation as one of the greatest relief pitchers of all time. He thrilled to tense situations in a baseball game. When the bases were loaded, with nobody out and the game at stake in the last inning, Joe Page would come in. He would take the mound relaxed and poised and his confidence was communicated to his teammates. The whole team steadied when Joe Page stepped onto the mound. His poise and his confidence came from his unique ability to ignore what did not matter. He was utterly indifferent toward men on the bases, except to see that nobody stole a base. So far as Mr. Page was concerned, there was only one problem—the man with the bat. The men on the bases were incapable of doing any damage whatever so long as he could manage the man with the bat. He ignored the unimportant factors in his situation.

Much of the nervous, bustling tension of our lives comes from our failure to see the difference between what matters and what does not. It comes from not sitting quietly now and then to think, and to see life in perspective. Henry Drummond used to say that he could manage the hurry and the rush of any day fate could bring if he could take just ten minutes of the day to be thoughtfully with God. In ten minutes he could clear away the clutter. In ten minutes he could eliminate the unimportant. In ten minutes he could see his course and find resources to stay on it.

Under the pressure of life that goes on and on without stopping for quietness and thought, we are likely to be thoughtless, going off in all directions at once, in response to whatever emotional winds may blow. It is our thoughtlessness that leads us to most of the personal conflicts that generate inner tensions. Living under the sway of a heedless, turbulent culture, we slip easily into the habit of turning impersonal issues into personal quarrels. It takes at least a moment of pause to preserve the rule of reason and to thwart the riotous invasion of emotion. Stop! Think! lest impersonal issues turn into personal resentments generating destructive tensions.

One of the most subtle problems of family life is the usual habit of translating the impersonal into the personal until emotional tension becomes explosive. Consider the question of the family budget. Money is impersonal, but money matters very easily turn into personal emotional problems. I suspect, after years of counseling with people, that more conflicts between husbands and wives arise over the use of money than over any other single issue. Observe what often happens. When there is no money in the family budget to buy a new fishing rod which "he" wants, "he" assumes "she" is being contrary. The fact that an impersonal budget will not stretch expresses itself in the comment: "She just doesn't want me to go fishing." That is nonsense. Stop! Think! When Johnny tears his new pants and new curtains must be deferred so that Johnny's nakedness can be covered, "she" says to Johnny: "You certainly don't love me, or you wouldn't play baseball in your new suit." That, on reflection, is ridiculous. Johnny was just being Johnny.

When we feel the pressure of expenses the budget will not cover, it always is a temptation to turn an impersonal fact into a personal hurt. The inevitable result is conflict in family relationships and emotional tensions that intensify the conflict. Actually, hard facts are hard facts, to be dealt with as such. The fact that there is not enough money for a new dishwasher if the insurance is to be kept up is a simple fact of arithmetic. It is fatal to turn a fact of arithmetic into the hurt emotional outburst, "You just don't want me to have a dishwasher."

If we would take time to think, to get our emotions under the control of our good sense, we would not turn impersonal problems into personal quarrels. We could avoid no end of strain. A college president put the matter succinctly when he was seeking to revise the curriculum of the institution and had run into a phalanx of faculty opposition. Said he: "I need perspective and constant prayer, because I know my major problem is myself." He went on to say: "One thing is plain: I must not allow academic issues to become personal quarrels." Exactly so. Academic issues can be met and creative solutions found for them if they remain academic issues, but the moment they become personal quarrels they become insoluble and the source of critical inner tensions.

There is a striking illustration of the truth in the experience of a visitor to China some years ago who came upon two Chinese arguing furiously, surrounded by a crowd. "What's going on?" he asked. "Oh, they are fighting," came the answer from an onlooker. Since no blows were being struck, the traveler inquired, "How come?" "Well," the onlooker replied, "the first man to strike a blow loses the fight. He admits that he has run out of ideas." In the same fashion, when we allow our emotions to dominate our reason and translate impersonal problems into personal quarrels we confess we have run out of ideas. Obviously, when we run out of ideas and begin to quarrel we find ourselves in the grip of perilous emotional tension. Stop! Think!

It is plain that if we are to order our lives and manage our tensions creatively, we need resources even beyond planning, resting, playing, and thinking. Our secular answers to the problem of tension are not enough, and as William Cowper noted, we need a defense against:

> . . . dropping buckets into empty wells
> And growing old in drawing nothing up.[2]

When we look into ourselves it is plain we are growing old drawing up too much of nothing.

Inner quietness in the face of outward pressure has its source in what might be called spiritual "change of pace." Arnold Toynbee notes our need for "withdrawal" and "return," for an Upper Room on Main Street so that we are able to move

> Up from the world of the many,
> To the over-world of the One.
> Back to the world of the many
> From the over-world of the One.[3]

Life demands periods of quietness in which we drop our buckets into wells of power and peace. It is in such moments that we learn what the Psalmist meant when he wrote of God that "He restores my soul."[4]

Fifteen or twenty minutes of quiet meditation and thought each day may bother you at first. It will seem like a waste of precious time. It seemed so to Southey, the British statesman, who thought it was a sin not to be active. He was talking on one occasion with a Quaker, describing how his days were filled, what he had to do from hour to hour. "But, friend Southey," the Quaker asked, "when dost thou think?" Apparently it had not occurred to Southey that meditation and thought were important. But Pascal notes that "All the evils of life have fallen upon us because men will not sit quietly in a room." And President Conant, of Harvard University, echoed the same conviction in his observation that all men need "the quiet privilege of an ivory tower."

There is a principle of alternation that seems to be a law of life. There is need for both driving ahead and pausing to find the way, for movement and for meditation. The archer hits his target both by pulling and by letting go. He brings the bow to stern tension and then lets it relax. The story is told of an old negress who put the idea humorously when she remarked: "When I works, I works hard. When I sets, I sets loose." It is the "setting loose" in relaxed quietness that is our need, for there is a relaxed and yet focused indolence that is the key to insight and to inner peace.

The mind has to "set loose" in quietness now and then to give God a chance. Paradoxically enough, when we strain less, God does more. I do not mean to suggest that we can just sit down on our shovels and let God do everything. On the contrary, there is what Karl Barth calls "a rest in battle," a pause that renews, a silence that inspires. Jesus found it when he retreated from his ministry to the wilderness and then returned "in the power of the spirit unto Galilee."[5] He went off into the Garden of Gethsemane, but when he came back, "the appearance of his countenance was altered";[6] tension and weariness were gone and serenity and peace were written there.

Life becomes stale, dead, and uncreative in everlasting tension. We become lost in the limbo of our frustrations and irritations without times of quietness when we rest back upon the buoyant strength of "the everlasting arms." "Be still and know that I am God"[7] was the Psalmist's way of describing his "rest in battle." "Come unto me, all ye that labor and are heavy laden and I will give you rest" was the Master's invitation to the tense and nervous. When you have squeezed all you are able from your mind and spirit, when you can't go on and you can't stop, there is a source of never-ending strength and peace in the silence with God. When you have been dropping buckets into empty wells until you are weary of it all, there are wells of living water in the quietness with God.

"The peace of God that passes all understanding"[8] is not an endless rest in fields "knee deep in clover." It is rather a profound inner trust that "in Him who strengthens me, I am able for anything."[9] It is assurance of inner adequacy. It is poise in the midst of panic and serenity in the midst of struggle. It is faith to say, "Even though I walk through the valley of the shadow of death, I fear no evil, for thou art with me."[10] Such assurance and peace come in moments of relaxed indolence with God.

Usually we need a little help to provide the mood for meditation that will set us free from tension. Happily, there is a well of faith and insight that never goes dry. It has been there on your table as long as you can remember, and most of the pages are still stuck together. You have a vague idea what is in it. There is a story about Daniel in the den of lions. Probably it has not occurred to you that you are very much like Daniel, except that Daniel had a thing called peace even when the lions roared and threatened his destruction. Then, too, there is the story about a pearl merchant, who had everything except the thing he wanted most, a bit of peace in the Kingdom of God. He is a reasonable facsimile of yourself. Maybe you had not noticed.

It is not your duty to read the Book of the Ages; it is your privilege. Of course, you can spend three dollars and buy a book telling you how to stop worrying, how to find peace of mind, or how to be sublimely confident. The book may help. It is modern and up to date, but it won't do half so much good as an excursion into the Psalms, from which the peace of God flows. You can buy a "how-to-do-it" magazine full of psychological tips on self-management, and it won't do you any harm. But John's Gospel, rich with the fragrance of Galilean hills, will leave you richer and better. Somehow, "the light" still "shines in darkness, and the darkness has not overcome it."[11]

There is a wonderful passage in Isaiah that might well have been written just for us:

Ho, everyone that thirsts, come to the waters, and he who has no money, come ye, buy and eat; come buy wine and milk without money and without price. Wherefore do you spend money for that which is not bread? and your labor for that which does not satisfy?[12]

Why drop buckets into empty wells when there is a well that is full of just what you need? Why run hither and yon trying to escape tension and strain when what you need most is on the table beside your bed?

Tomorrow morning your tension will be creative if tonight you gather "quietness and confidence" from the "pages of power." Life demands capacity for tension, the keyed-up energy of the executive and the salesman, but the capacity for creative tension tomorrow is born in the knowledge that tonight "He restores my soul."[13] General Gordon knew the truth when he stood alone in Egypt, literally praying his boats up the Nile

River, and finding the only peace there was in the midst of war in his worn Bible. The dynamic for tomorrow always is born in the peace of tonight that flows from the "old, old story."

Many a man has come to the end of his rope, knowing he could not go on and he could not stop, and then in the desperation of need dropped his bucket into the well that never goes dry, only to discover a solid knot on the end of the rope and strength to hang on forever. Woodrow Wilson, through all the stormy years of his life, found peace in the Scriptures and capacity for frightful strain even when friends and colleagues failed him. Tonight you can find peace and poise for tomorrow's tension.

Of course, if you expect to find help in the pages of Scripture, you have to be more than casual about your reading. There is more than a little wisdom in the observation of Somerset Maugham that the reader of a novel owes something to the novelist.[14] No writer, however skillful, can capture the casual or the inattentive. The reader owes the novelist enough application to read the novel through. What is more, he owes the novelist enough imagination to visualize the characters who walk through the pages of a book, enough imagination to enter into the setting of the novel with understanding. Finally, the reader owes the writer enough sympathy to share the feelings of the characters who plod along in print, to feel their fears, their hurts, their joys, and their passions.

Obviously, you owe something to the saints and seers who composed the Scriptures. That is, you owe them something if you expect them to give you anything in return. Certainly you owe them the courtesy of a hearing, the application required to read what they wrote with the "blood, sweat and tears" of their lives. You owe them the use of your imagination too, so that Abraham, Isaac, and Jacob become more than names. You have to fill in the picture so that they become at least as real as

George Washington or Abraham Lincoln. Peter and Paul and Jesus need to come alive in your mind so that they preach and teach and suffer like real people. Then, of course, you owe the writers of the Book of the Ages enough sympathy to enter into their experience. If you feel the yearning of the Psalmists you will also find the peace they found. If you feel the need of Zacchaeus, you will find the courage that came to him. If you feel the love of the Master breathing through his parables, you will find what the saints have found in him.

Just flipping the pages of the Bible will not help. Just reading words that do not penetrate beneath the surface will leave you unrelieved. It is entering into the spirit of the book and letting God speak through it to you and your need that makes the difference. You can drink deeply of the living waters if you will, and they will refresh your soul. You can pause "beside the still waters" of God and come away in peace, the tensions of your life eased. The price is application, imagination, sympathy.

When men from among "the vast cloud of witnesses" speak to you from the Pages of Power, you begin to see your job and your burdens in perspective. When God speaks to you through them, life takes on a new pattern. You see the difference between main issues and sheer clutter. You are able to plan your days purposefully and erase the secondary while you address yourself to the primary. When there is peace inside, what is outside can be taken in stride. When your mind is focused in the quietness, it is clear and precise under pressure.

Then, too, the moments of quietness with God speaking through the Scriptures bring release from tension by infusing life with meaning and purpose. To be significant, to mean something, to be doing something that matters is essential to our inner poise. Tension comes out of toiling furiously for nothing in particular. Life flows easily when it is guided by a sure sense of direction. When we see ourselves bearing torches in the service of God's eternal purpose, we do not throw up our hands in the face of conflict or pressure, muttering: "What's the use?" On the contrary, we face our experience saying: "This is worth fighting for."

James Ramsey Ullman, famous mountain climber and author of the novel *The White Tower,* describes his experience introducing his two sons, Jim, eight years old, and Bill, six, to mountain climbing.[15] They started with Mount Dunderberg, a modest mountain in the Hudson River Highlands. Almost from the beginning the two boys reacted differently to the climb. Jim was eager, curious, excited. Bill wanted none of it. With each turn of the trail, Bill's pace grew slower and his expression more grimly tense. First he fell on his face and then he sat down with a grunt. He tore his jacket, scraped his knees, and came off second best in a brush with a thornbush. For a while he withheld comment, but presently the time came when he could keep his question back no longer. "Dad," he asked, raising a puzzled face, "are we doing this for fun?"

That, of course, was the sixty-four-dollar question. Climbing was fun for Jim and his dad, but it was sheer drudgery for poor Bill, and all the discussion in the world would not change his mind about it. Tense, frustrated, irritated, he plodded on convinced it was nonsense. Jim and his dad were challenged by the mountain. Here was something to be mastered; here were heights to be achieved. The mountain held beauties to be seen, wild flowers, twisted trees, and a glorious panorama to be viewed from its crest. Climbing was purposeful for Jim and his dad. There was release, freedom, and fun in it. Not so for Bill; he wanted to quit, to go home, to stop where he was.

The Christian faith puts purpose into life. By the light of it, problems become opportunities for insight. In the quietness with God, hardships become growing points, and difficulties become sources of dynamic. We cannot be tense and flustered when we are climbing for a purpose and using our climbing to strengthen our muscles and broaden our vision. We cannot be bursting with strain when we find the purpose of our lives in the fact that under the pressure of life we are fashioning our souls and growing in spiritual and moral stature.

There is a "rest in battle," a "withdrawal" into the presence of God that yields perspective and meaning to relieve the tension of our days. St. Paul knew the truth when he wrote to the Philippians. He was not writing nonsense from his prison cell when he promised that "the peace of God that passes all understanding will keep your hearts and minds in Christ Jesus."[16] He knew what tension meant. He had heard the angry mobs clamoring for his life. He had felt stones crashing into his body as mobs sought to kill him on the spot. He had been through shipwreck and the stark terror of storms at sea. He had felt the brutal hurt of the cat-o'-nine-tails on his naked back. Paul lived in tension all his life, but he had found a priceless "rest in battle." He knew "the power of God for salvation"[17] that would see him through, and he knew in the midst of it all what was vital. In the quietness he had found "the peace of God that passes all understanding."

Along the road that leads to the peace of God there are a multitude of trivial imps. Indeed, many of the tensions we meet are fashioned from trifles. Our faith to manage our lives, therefore, constrains us to consider the trifles that need to be put in their proper place.

CHAPTER VI

Putting Trifles in Their Place

SOMETIMES our tensions are inspired by trifles that have an irritating habit of rushing on to life's stage and stealing the show. A flat tire when you start for work on a bright, sunny morning can ruin your day. A small boy's accident, spilling milk at the breakfast table, can play havoc with your disposition and leave you a twelve-hour legacy of irritability. The fact that Mrs. Smith neglected to invite you to her luncheon is quite likely to leave you out of sorts, if not angry, for a week. When you have time to get a bit of perspective, it is perfectly clear that the flat tire, the spilled milk, and the luncheon were trifles, not really worth ten minutes' concern. Nevertheless, they stole the show and made you miserable.

In George Santayana's novel *The Last Puritan,* one of the characters remarks: "Ah, the little troubles, Mr. Oliver, they ruin a woman's life"[1]—and, one might add, a man's life too. The price of butter and eggs, and Willie's torn trousers assume the proportions of catastrophe and leave us breathless. The "little troubles" upset our digestion and give us ulcers when in reality they should not trouble us more than a moment. Trifles keep us awake half the night and mole hills turn into mountains before morning. Geared to little things, our lives become as small as our little troubles. Trifles rob us of our power to live creatively and richly.

When you stop to consider the matter it is altogether absurd to allow trifles to pre-empt the stage. By definition a trifle is "a thing of little value or importance," a "paltry, trivial affair" that really is not worth more than a moment's notice. Nevertheless, trifles do invade our lives to obscure the primary business of living. They are one of life's annoying inevitables and we have no choice but to accept their undesired company. They are paltry and they are unimportant, but there they are, as inescapable as your face when you look into a mirror.

In dealing with trifles and learning to manage them in stride it helps immeasurably simply to accept the fact that they are quite inevitable. Shoes squeak, doors bang, children spill milk, husbands snore, the television stops working, or the faucets drip to annoy you no matter how distinguished you may be. You haven't been singled out by an inconsiderate Providence to be annoyed. You are simply meeting life as it is. Nevertheless, we often complicate trifles by assuming we run into more of them than anyone else does. We give vent to our feeling when we say: "Why does something like this always have to happen to me?"

Annoyances confront all of us, not just you. Mention the way your husband leaves his clothes scattered over the room instead of hanging them where they belong the next time you meet at your club and listen to the chorus. "My husband tramps in from the garden with mud on his feet until I want to scream." Or "My husband leaves his cigar butts scattered all over the house." "My husband . . . ," and so on until it is plain that in one way or another what happens to you happens to everybody.

Listen to a crowd of high-school youngsters, upset by trifles. One says, "Mother made me wear my galoshes. I'm so mad." Another remarks angrily, "My father says I've got to be home by midnight tonight. It's just unfair." "My parents won't let me have the car. How can I have any fun?" It really is not important one way or the other, not important enough to ruin a day or a party. Annoying things happen day after day and year after year, and sooner or later we must come to terms with the trifles that keep us in emotional turmoil and seething with anger and resentment.

When we quietly confront the fact that the intrusion of annoying trifles is inevitable, it is helpful to recognize that there are some trivial imps that can be eliminated and some others we cannot escape. Some are permanent; whether we like it or not we have to learn to live with them. Some years ago, for example, a permanent imp undertook to push me around. The Evanston city police put up two-hour parking signs all around my neighborhood, even across the street. That seemed quite reasonable until all-day parkers began to park in front of my house. They filled the whole side of the street from corner to corner. I would come home from taking my sons to school and at eight-thirty o'clock I could not find a place to park. My blood pressure went up several points each morning. I thought I would put up a sign, but one of my neighbors tried it and it did not work. One morning I called out the window to a would-be parker asking him not to block my entrance. He gave me a glassy stare and walked off without moving his car an inch.

There were several possibilities open in that situation. I could let my children walk to school and park my car in front of my house early enough to thwart the trespassers. I could complain to the police and probably get a polite brushoff. I could make myself obnoxious defending my imagined rights each morning. Or I could accept the irritation as a permanent annoying trifle and make it a habit to park in the garage in the alley. After some inner struggle I adopted the last course and simply ignored the cars in front of my house. With a bit of rationalizing

I persuaded myself that the car was safer and better off in the garage than in front of the house.

In dealing with myself and the problem of parking, I got some practical help from George Washington Carver, who was in charge of the buildings and grounds at Tuskegee Institute. The grass on the campus was his pride and joy. Being an artist in spirit, he had laid out the walks with an eye to the most harmonious arrangement. Then the students and faculty members, instead of walking where they should have walked, would make straight for their objective regardless of the grass. "Don't walk on the grass" signs seemed to invite defiance. Annoyed, Dr. Carver made announcements requesting respect for the grass. He got nowhere. He was becoming upset and peevish, so he delivered a lecture to himself: "Why waste time getting perturbed and accomplishing nothing? People are going to travel in a way that is logical."[2] So he sat down and watched the way people walked and then put paths under their feet. Thereafter, he observed with satisfaction that they stayed on them.

Obviously there are times when you have no choice except to adjust to your irritations in such fashion that they cease to be irritations. There is no use being stubborn about things you cannot change. The result is simply permanent frustration.

Of course, irritating trifles should not be accepted when it is possible to do something about them. You need to learn to recognize the difference between trivial annoyances that need to be accepted and those that can be eliminated at their source. Columnist Robert C. Ruark, for example, says he is annoyed by pigeons. A pigeon "doesn't even know how to make a proper nest"; it is "the untidiest critter" he knows. He insists that pigeon offspring "are the most repulsive looking monsters in the juvenile stage." The whole pigeon tribe is "arrogant," offensive, and good for nothing. Pigeons clutter the streets and sidewalks and look offended if you disturb them. So Mr. Ruark undertook to express his annoyance by kicking a pigeon. It was not at all satisfying, he notes, since it was like "slugging a sponge." He remarks in conclusion: "There are so many elusive annoyances that need a boot in the tail, and the opportunity occurs too seldom."

Mr. Ruark may be right, but I strongly suspect that kicking annoyances you cannot avoid only begets more annoyances and the last state is worse than the first. Pigeons, if you do not like them, are in the same category as cars parked in front of your house or walks people will not use. They have to be accepted. They breed faster than you can kick them or kill them off. Kick one pigeon and there are still plenty left to elude your foot.

On the other hand, there are annoying trifles you can eliminate. Take the Sunday paper, for example. I like to read the Sunday paper, but it annoys me to find it scattered all over the house as if a tornado had hit it. I like to find it all in one bundle the way it came, but my three boys seem to care not at all what happens to it. On numerous occasions I have exploded all over the house. However, I must confess that when I finished with the paper it was somewhat disheveled. We finally got together and decided that the Sunday paper was a family institution. Therefore, whoever read it was responsible for putting it together for the next reader. We eliminated a trivial irritation at its source.

There are times when a little personal discipline can get rid of annoying trifles. Children habitually late for dinner can be cured by having their allowance docked, and fathers who never think to hang up their clothes can be cured by the simple process of having to pay a quarter into the family piggy bank, thus relieving mother's irritation. A little imagination can go a long way toward eliminating a host of disturbing trifles in family life, making living happier and richer. Take a look around you at the trifles that bother you and at yourself to discover the things you do that annoy others and you will discover that many of them can be avoided with a little thoughtfulness and consideration. Obviously, you need to be sensitive to people and the things that upset them, eager to find ways and means of curing what can be cured and adjusting to what cannot be changed. Kicking pigeons is a last resort!

It should be noted that, no matter what the irritation, a sense of humor is a saving virtue. It helps immeasurably when little things are beginning to get on your nerves. Years ago, for example, there used to be a hoot owl that habitually hooted in a tree outside the window of my summer cottage. I would turn off the light and settle down for a warm, comfortable sleep, and I would be greeted with "whoo, whoo" shattering the incredible silence of night in the mountains. Of course, the owl was simply being an owl, and I suppose his particular tree was as important to him as my bed was to me. But I wished he would be an owl somewhere else. One night I got up and chased him out of his tree with a rock, but before I could get back into bed he was there again, "whoo-whooing" at me.

Then, to make matters worse, I discovered that my wife was laughing. At the moment, nothing seemed funny, but as the owl gave vent to its annoyance by whooing furiously, it did seem funny and my wife and I had a good laugh together. Thereafter, I promptly went to sleep despite the owl, and now I can't seem to remember whether or not the owl went on hooting the rest of the night. A hearty laugh overwhelmed the unimportance of a trivial annoyance and put it in its place.

Humor can be invaluable as an instrument for bringing our ridiculous selves under control. When trifles throw us into a tailspin it is sometimes indicative of the fact that we are taking ourselves much too seriously. After all, the world was not organized altogether for my own benefit, and I suppose owls do have some rights in the natural scheme of things, even when they happen to be annoying to me. There is no use in being serious and grim over owls of one sort or another. Muriel Lester remarks that, no matter what annoyances intrude upon her days, she has learned never to be "grim on God's errands gay." She knows full well that in every irritation there is the possibility of gaiety, and that God's great errand of living ought to be joyous.

Time and again Abraham Lincoln escaped the tension of petty irritations by seeing the possibility of gaiety in them. When cartoonists caricatured him unkindly, he could chuckle over his own homeliness, wishing that if God ever made a homelier man he might meet him. He read passages from Artemas Ward, the great American humorist, to his cabinet when tempers were on edge. When his children irritated him with their petty quarrels, he found the humor in the situation. His sense of humor was a safety valve he opened to relieve pressure and to translate grimness into gaiety.

Not to be able to laugh at ourselves and our petty irritations suggests a hardening of the arteries of good humor. It is tragic to be like Benjamin, the oldest animal on "Animal Farm," pictured with delightful satire by George Orwell. Benjamin was thoroughly bad tempered. Everything annoyed him in his ultra-serious sobriety. When he talked, it was usually to make some cynical remark. He would say, for instance, that "God had given him a tail to keep the flies off, but he would sooner have no tail and no flies."[3] Alone among the animals on the farm, he never laughed. "If asked why, he would say that he saw nothing to laugh at." But to see nothing to laugh at in our upsetting irritations invites seething resentment.

There is more than a little wisdom in the comment of a small boy who ran into a rock with his tricycle and fell off. He burst out laughing, and a passer-by asked: "Why on earth are you laughing?" The boy answered: "I am laughing so that I won't

cry." There are times when we need to laugh so that we will
not lose our self-possession; to chuckle over our own irritations
so that we will not boil over in frustrated anger. Laughter is a
remarkable safety valve in the face of irritated indignation.

Whether you laugh or cry, boil over or manage your irritations at the moment, at least put them to bed and lay them to
rest before you turn in for the night. "Let not the sun go down
on thy wrath" is the essence of wisdom. As William Osler wrote
long years ago, "The petty annoyances, the real and fancied
slights, the trivial mistakes, the disappointments, the sins, the
sorrows, even the joys—bury them deep in the oblivion of each
night."[4] Unhappily, it is just then that the ghosts come trooping
into our minds, pry open our eyelids, and keep us twisting and
turning through the long watches of the dark. We need to undress our minds as we undress our bodies, quietly shedding the
garmenture of the day when we retreat into the night. Change
your mind when you change into your night clothes. It is as
foolish to wear your out-of-press, wrinkled irritations to bed
as to crawl in between the sheets with your clothes on.

To be sure, undressing your mind requires some discipline,
the introduction of fresh ideas and new thoughts. Even a mystery story, if it does not stimulate you too much, can be a help.
A friend of mine reads a bit of Plato each night. He finds a
sense of the eternal in the serenity of philosophy, something
to tie his mind to what is important. My wife signs off the day
with poetry that sounds a hopeful, encouraging note and so
pushes out the cobwebs of irritation and annoyance. A man I
know has a record player beside his bed. Each night he plays
"Ave Maria" and "The Lord's Prayer" after he turns out the
light. They put his mind in a quiet, reverent mood, and trivialities are lost in the deeps of God.

The habit of devotional reading, meditation, and prayer when
the fever of the day is done is a vital and a fruitful way of un-

dressing the mind and leaving the weight of irritations behind. It is a strange fact that a great Psalm, surrounding our littleness with a sense of the everlasting, can banish the troubling trifles and put them in their place. Under the benediction of spiritual reality, "He giveth his beloved sleep." In the moments when we lose ourselves in the quietness of the Sermon on the Mount, the mind comes to rest in the wonder of God. The sweeping cadences of the Lord's Prayer, "Our Father, who art in heaven," reverently uttered sweep out the dusty corners of our minds where irritations fester and breed insomnia.

Tomorrow will be cluttered with yesterday's trifles if you take little annoyances to bed with you to destroy your sleep. But tomorrow can be better than today if you undress your mind before you turn out the light for the night. Mrs. William Carey Brownell pays tribute to the "masculine largeness" of her husband, who habitually let "minor matters take care of themselves" and would drop off to sleep quietly "in the midst of situations that would keep a woman awake half the night." He habitually "washed his brain" with the cleansing spirit of God and quickly found the wonder of sleep. Go thou and do likewise.

The basic problem in dealing with trivialities at the moment we meet them is to keep our perspective. Commonly our irritations lower our horizons so that nothing appears on the screen our minds see except the irritations. Values and possibilities are blotted out and both the mind and the emotions are saturated in resentful annoyance. So we are candidates for further annoyance by petty frustrations. Trouble "comes in bunches," we say, and so do irritations. When we are resentfully annoyed by spilled milk, we are emotionally in the market for a quarrel with the grocery boy who forgot to bring the loaf of bread we ordered. When we are irritated by a wrong number on the telephone, we are ripe to be thoroughly upset by the unexpected guest who came to dinner. When we cannot see anything but our irritations, we develop moods that are susceptible to more irritations. Little troubles always are an invitation to more little troubles unless we are able to handle them without losing perspective.

Of course, there are times when annoying trifles pile up on us, willy-nilly, without rhyme or reason. One annoyance has no particular causal relation to another, except that each succeeding petty event adds to our problem. Mrs. Miniver understood her need for perspective as she went about her household duties and met succeeding petty problems. As a rule she managed to keep household matters in what she considered their proper place.

They should be no more, she felt, than a low unobtrusive humming in the background of consciousness: the mechanics of life never should be allowed to interfere with living. But every now and then, everything went wrong at once, chimneys smoked, pipes burst, vacuum cleaners fused, china and glassware fell to pieces, net curtains disintegrated in the wash. Nannie sprained her ankle, the cook got tonsillitis, the parlor maid left to be married, and the butterfly nut off the mincing machine was nowhere to be found.[5]

Like Mrs. Miniver you may be able to manage one or two distractions without going to pieces with the nervous jitters. But when the lace curtains disintegrate at the same time the chimney smokes and the pipes burst, it is just too much. They add up to a bad case of nerves. When trifle is piled on trifle, you become their victim. What happens is clear enough. You lose your perspective. Your horizons come down to zero. You cannot see anything but burst pipes and smoking chimneys. It is like fog rolling in to obscure the road ahead, the sky above, and the scenery on the right and on the left. You are left in a miserable little world of two-by-four dimensions, utterly filled with annoyances.

Under the circumstances, the admonition of Isaiah is of the utmost importance: "Get you up to a high mountain"[6] to regain perspective. There are some positives in the situation and you can see them from a mountain's vantage point. You still have a home to live in, even though the chimney smokes, and if you are lucky enough to have a cook, you are better off than most people, even though the cook may have tonsillitis. Spilled milk may be annoying, but it is not a disaster. You still have a bottle or two in the refrigerator, and there are plenty of people in the world who have neither refrigerators nor milk. Johnny may be upsetting at times, but you do have Johnny, and life would be empty without him. If the china falls to pieces, there is a dime store around the corner, and broken china is not a tragedy anyway. It is trivial beside a lot of other things. "Get you up to a high mountain."

You may need a little time out to climb the high mountain. It takes time—and discipline, too—to climb the Matterhorn, and it takes time to climb mountains of the spirit from which to view our lives and experiences in perspective. Take a hint from the Psalmist of old: "I lift up my eyes to the hills,"[7] above the plodding march of the days, for "my help comes from the Lord."[8] Mrs. Miniver described her experience of climbing the high mountain in a down-to-earth fashion, when she noted that in times of irritation "you just put on spiritual dungarees and remain in them until things are running smoothly again."[9] Spiritual overalls will do as well for the men when it is flat tires or dull-witted office boys who are the source of the trouble. A few well-chosen verses of Scripture help amazingly when you are trying to put on spiritual dungarees, or get to some mountain for new perspective. "Be still and know that I am God,"[10] or "Thou dost keep him in perfect peace whose mind is stayed on Thee,"[11] or "In all your ways acknowledge him, and he will make straight your paths,"[12] repeated mentally, will work wonders. They are far more serviceable than the usual outburst of profanity. A simple prayer, "O God, give me grace to remain serene," will broaden your horizons and get you out of the two-by-four world of your irritations. Bring God into your upset situation and you will find yourself on a mountain, seeing things in better proportion.

The vantage point of your spiritual mountain, for one thing, will enable you to sense that life's most important values often are nourished on the creative use of annoying trifles. Indeed, it takes the moral equivalent of a lost butterfly nut to feed our patience. We cannot "grow in grace" on a diet of strawberries and cream. It takes hardtack now and then to develop the digestive apparatus. That is why there would be a lot less grace and loveliness and fineness of character if it were not for obstreperous children who teach parents how to put up with annoyances and keep their spirits sweet in spite of them. If there were fewer burst pipes and smoking chimneys, there would be fewer saints.

If, from your spiritual mountaintop, you can see trifles in perspective you can get your money's worth from them. You will see them as growing points on the road to mature selfhood. You will comprehend them as they can be, as tools with which to fashion character. Indeed, the great enterprise of your life, the fashioning of your own soul, requires the tempering of annoying trifles. But unless you are aware both of the great enterprise and of the creative possibilities of petty annoyances you will not manage yourself sanely in upsetting situations. Take time out, therefore, and "get you up to a high mountain."

Almost any annoying situation you can imagine contains possibilities of growth either for you or for someone whose life touches yours. Take your children, for example. They are a bother at times, inescapably so. They are forever asking silly questions when you are trying to rest. They want you to play blocks or baseball when you want to read the paper. They get into mischief, spilling flour or sugar on the kitchen floor, and you feel as if you would like to scream. But if you have your eyes fixed on what you are trying to do with and for your children it helps wonderfully. If you are seeking to create character and train them to bear the weight of their own independence, even the annoying interruptions are teaching opportunities. Spilled food is a chance to demonstrate the importance of patience. Playing blocks when you would rather read the paper can be a means of demonstrating that building anything demands solid foundations. You can take interruptions in your stride if you have learned to use them as growing points.

Time and again I have been in the midst of writing a sermon, only to be interrupted by some annoying trifle. By the time I get back to the sermon, the idea that seemed so vital has slipped from my mind. It is exasperating. Why can't people leave me alone while I am writing? Then, when I stop to think, it is plain that people are my business. Their problems ought to be my problems, their hurts my hurts. After all, sermons grow out of the everyday problems of ordinary people, and ordinary people are interrupted and annoyed. "Physician, heal thyself." So I am learning as the years go by to remember that people are my business. If they interrupt me, they do so because to them what they want is important. What is more, times without number interruptions have resulted in creative insights that have been aids in preaching to the needs of people.

Keep your mind focused in the faith that even annoyances can be instruments of the great enterprise. They are worth enduring if they teach you to be patient. They are worth what they cost in time and effort if you use them to teach others something they ought to know. Never forget that every life experience, no matter how distasteful, can be a source of personal growth and power. A young G.I. expressed the idea: "I was irritated and annoyed when the draft board called me," he said. "At first I hated the army and everything about it, and life was miserable. Then I decided I was being foolish. So, when I landed in Japan I decided to learn Japanese. I spent all my spare time studying, and in eighteen months, I learned to speak and to write Japanese. Now the State Department has offered me a good job in Washington."

The problem of life is to keep your mind focused on the great conviction that no annoyance or interruption you meet is too large or too small to contribute something to the sum total of yourself. If the great enterprise of living is to make the most of your own possibilities of mind and spirit and character, then you can take whatever touches your life and use it creatively. The imps that annoy you can minister to your character. The demons that interrupt you can add to your spiritual stature. But clearly, what you do with the trifles or the big things that disturb your elected course depends upon perspective enough to see them in relation to the vital enterprise of your life.

There is a sense in which life is like walking across a very narrow bridge over a roaring river. If you watch your feet you will grow dizzy and lose your balance. Safety lies in fixing your gaze upon a knot in a tree or some fixed point on the other side. Rivet your eyes on some steadying point where you are going and you will travel the narrow bridge with sure steps. So life demands a steadying goal across the chasms we must traverse, a vital undertaking on the far horizon beyond the trivial troubles that beset our days.

The steadying enterprise that sends you through the days resolved to translate experience into character performs a function similar to that of the mechanism in the human body that keeps its temperature constant. It makes no difference what the reading of the thermometer outside is, the inner temperature remains at approximately 98.6 degrees. Zero outside leaves the body temperature unaltered. A blistering 110 degrees in the shade makes no change in the temperature inside. You may shiver or sweat, but unless illness strikes you, your body temperature remains at approximately 98.6 degrees. Just so, the purpose beyond the immediate irritations helps to stabilize your emotional temperature.

There is a word of negative wisdom in *The Screwtape Letters,* by C. S. Lewis. Screwtape, an undersecretary in hell, is charged with the task of supervising a certain client until he arrives safely in hell at the end of his earthly life. Each time the demoniac missionary gets into trouble, he writes the underworld for advice, and the book is a collection of the letters of counsel sent to him. On one occasion the earthly demon is in trouble because his client has joined the church. "Now what do we do?" he wants to know. Satan replies that the matter is not as serious as it seems. He counsels his emissary on earth to be sure to keep with his patient at all times, especially in church. When in church, "keep him aware of little things"—of the fact that this usher is a hypocrite, that this man's shoes squeak, that this lady's hat does not fit properly. Keep him aware of little things, and never, never "let him see the church with her banners flying for that is a sight at which all hell trembles."[13]

It is the church with all her banners flying that gives meaning to our participation in it, and it is our devotion to the great enterprise of life with all its banners flying that gives meaning to our life's struggle through the maze of irritating trifles. Ray Stannard Baker once received a letter from a woman in New York which suggests our need for some sense of meaning while we struggle on from day to day. She was the mother of six children ranging in age from six months to twenty years. So much to do. She had to stop "between every three words to straighten a wobbly baby in her pillows on the floor." "Your books," she wrote, "give me courage and comfort and help me to take things as they come, minute by minute." Then she put her finger on our need for "some acknowledgement that all my weariness and effort pays."[14]

Weariness and effort and the minute-by-minute struggle with trivial problems are worth what they cost if we are able to comprehend their meaning in terms of their contribution to life's great enterprise. They are utterly futile and worthy only of resentment if they contribute nothing to our maturity. But they do have meaning. You can push on confident that the end justifies the struggle and strain of little troubles and big ones too. Such confidence is a necessary ingredient in all great living. You cannot manage trifles without it. They will get the best of you as sure as fate. So keep your eyes fixed on the great enterprise of fashioning your soul after the very image of Christ and you will manage your irritations creatively.

Trifles tremble and lose their power to upset us when they have meaning in terms of a maturing life committed to a significant goal. The secret of John Wesley's power, said Quiller-Couch, was "his kingly neglect of trifles." He could ignore the little irritations that would keep most people awake half the night. He could endure uncomfortable inns, the frustration of a lame horse, the cantankerousness of liverymen, with quiet poise. After all, these were little things that had no business getting in the way of the stirring enterprise of his life. These were things to be mastered, rather than to be his master. With "kingly neglect of trifles" he pushed on with his work. Nothing must get in the way of his major business. Everything would be lost if a greasy breakfast in a dirty inn ruined his disposition and spoiled a sermon!

Henry Beetle Hough suggests the importance of finding meaning for life and for work in terms of some guiding purpose or meaningful goal. He describes the problem of editing a small-town newspaper, and the story is revealing because it shows so clearly how meaning goes out of writing and working when an editor loses sight of his function. "If you don't watch out," Mr. Hough writes, "a country newspaper will edit itself . . . and when the paper is out the editors will wonder what happened to the good intentions with which they began the week."[15] Life is like that. If you do not keep your eyes fixed on the great enterprise, life will "edit itself" and lose its meaning. You will be just putty in the hands of your frustrations and irritations. Your intentions will become tangled and lost in a web of trivial concerns until, when your day is done, you will wonder what on earth happened.

So it is that we need to withdraw now and then from the turbulent rush of the days to see ourselves and our experiences from the perspective of God. That is why the significance of at least weekly worship cannot be overestimated, for in worship you lift the whole of your life into the light of the ultimate and the abiding. You see both your irritations and the great enterprise of your life in the perspective of God. You pause in the presence of the Eternal to "see life steadily and see it whole." Your judgments in moments of worship are truer and your sense of values is sounder. Worship is akin to the experience of one of Napoleon's captains who went with the "Little Corporal" to Egypt, glorying in the invincible power of armies and men until one night he climbed to the top of a hill and looked out over the camp with its hundreds of tents shivering in the desert wind. Then his eyes fell upon the pyramids silhouetted against the night sky, mighty, silent, age old. The tents seemed puny then, and the blustering power of men appeared feeble and futile. So when we "lift our eyes unto the hills" in worship, we see with strange new insight what things are puny and trivial, what things ought to be set aside for the sake of values that are lasting.

There is a wonderful story of Plato's describing how Socrates

went to the Athenian fair, an exhibit of the gadgets and hand-
work of the golden fifth century before Christ. Everybody
seemed excited about the fair, its entertainment and its amuse-
ments, but Socrates shrugged his shoulders and remarked:
"There is so much here that I do not want." Somehow, the
sage of Athens had climbed above life's clutter like a man
worshiping in a cathedral, seeing things for what they really
are worth. He was not deceived by the trivial. Not even the
wagging tongue of Xantippe, his wife, could upset the steady
tempo of his life. He took the days in his stride and achieved a
"kingly neglect of trifles."

When your life has lost its focus and a motley collection of
trivial matters have left you confused, go into your church,
perhaps when no one is there. Let your eyes take in the altar
and the cross that honors the chancel. Let silence engulf your
spirit and lift your mind above the level of your plodding feet.
Little things will seem little then. Your stubbornness will seem
more like stubbornness and less like righteousness there in the
shadow of God. Your anger will soften under the brooding
light of Eternity. Trivial things that mattered so much an hour
before will seem not to matter at all. Resentments, accumulated
through days of irritation and annoyance, will fold their tents
and vanish. You will have no desire, then, to kick pigeons!

The wonder of worship is that it puts God at the center of
life. It is like standing in a valley and looking upward to the
crest of a high mountain peak. Maybe you have sand in your
shoes and a blister on your heel, but for a moment at least the
glory of the mountain makes you forget the sand and the
blister. Worship is like watching a sunset and forgetting your
headache or listening to a nightingale and being oblivious of
your neighbor's barking dog. It is strange how trivial irritations
cease to be irritating when you escape from yourself and are
lost in the wonder of God.

CHAPTER VII

Do You Feel Insecure?

IN OUR times the answer to the question "Do you feel insecure?" is another question: "Who doesn't?" No doubt historians of the future will call our times the era of anxiety and insecurity. It is ironic that we feel most insecure at a time when we are trying most desperately to provide "social security" for everybody. On the face of it, we ought to feel secure. We have been promised security in old age, security in unemployment, security in illness, but for all the promises we feel insecure. Paradoxically, we feel the insecurity of security. We have an uneasy suspicion that the promised security itself is insecure.

Our misgivings have been multiplied by world events that seem to be rushing toward an uncertain climax. They have been multiplied, too, by the suspicion that men cannot be trusted with power, and magnified by the uneasy feeling that we are quite helpless in the face of the gathering storm. We know all too well that many of the securities we have taken for granted are not as sound as we thought. Dollars are not dollars any more. They are only half-dollars. That has come as something of a shock. Gilt-edged bonds are not gilt edged any more. Nothing seems to have a really solid base in our times and we wonder if storms will sweep away the lovely houses we seem to have built on sand when we thought we were building on rock.

Our divided world, free and slave, scowling at itself across an Iron Curtain, has generated a climate of fear and suspicion. The race for supremacy in atomic weapons, the power of which to destroy us is beyond calculation, has inspired in us all a deep-seated anxiety. The stories of spies and subversives working to destroy the land we love have stirred us with anger and intensified our feeling of insecurity. Inevitably there have been those who have played on our fears in pursuit of political advantage. We read and listen to the news anxiously wondering what new treachery will be revealed until we suffer from bulletin biliousness and commentator cramps.

The insecurity we feel has exposed us to four dangers which undermine our capacity for self-management and creative living. The first danger is the disposition to make security the final value before which all other values bow. Under the stress of insecurity, we want to be safe. A recent television episode strikingly illustrated our contemporary mood. A goonlike character with a pug nose and an evil-looking face appeared on the screen. He was talking with a frightened, mousey little Mr. Milquetoast, threatening him with a booming voice: "If you know what's good for you, you won't say nuttin' to nobody."

"If you know what's good for you." The plain implication of the warning is that it is good to be safe, no matter what other values may be involved. It is better to keep still than to speak out against evil, better to play safe than to risk anything for righteousness. Under the stress of insecurity, security looms as the *summum bonum,* the primary good.

Voices everywhere are saying: "If you know what's good for you, you won't say anything that might possibly be construed as unpatriotic by some arch-defender of Americanism." "If you know what's good for you, you won't let your ideals get in the way of your politics." "Don't champion unpopular causes, even if you believe in them; you might get hurt." We identify the good with the secure, the safe, or the profitable and then blunder along doing what we think is good for us.

It is important to notice, however, that the great pioneers of human progress had a far more significant notion of what the good really means. When Columbus set sail in search of the East Indies the "wise" men of his time warned, "If you know what's good for you, you will stay home." But Columbus "sailed the ocean blue" in the strange conviction that it was good to explore the unknown even if it cost him his life.

Public opinion was decisively against Roger Williams when he argued for a fair deal for the American Indians and for religious liberty in the colonies. The preachers and the colonial leaders of his day told him bluntly, "If you know what's good for you, you will keep your opinions to yourself." But Roger Williams had a mind of his own and courage to risk the consequences of his convictions. He was driven from Salem, Massachusetts, into the wilderness in the middle of winter. Later he founded Providence, Rhode Island, and there laid foundations for the freedom that is ours today. He knew that it was good to be free, no matter what happened to him.

There are powerful forces in our time saying, "If you know what's good for you, you will conform." Indeed, there is a mob shouting for security, threatening the voices that are raised in defense of freedom and human dignity. We seem intent on destroying the "scoundrels" who do not think as we think, who do not say what we say. Liberals are dangerous. Anybody who will not conform in the name of security should be tarred and feathered.

So we blunder into the second danger of a time of insecurity.

We develop a mood of hostility toward those who seem to endanger our security. But hostility, once planted in the human spirit, has a habit of striking out without careful discrimination. Hating Communists too easily becomes hating anybody who dares to be different. Hostility refuses to stay put. It diffuses itself in all directions. It strikes out against Jews or foreigners or Negroes. It views life with suspicion and ranges class against class, labor against capital, and vice versa.

We even look with suspicion and hostility toward neighbors with whom we do not see eye to eye. Not long ago a thoughtful woman remarked: "We don't dare discuss political issues in our social group any more. Everybody gets mad." Who has not noticed the heat and hostility that are generated in political discussions, especially when Senator Joseph McCarthy is mentioned? Under the impact of our insecurity, we react to alien convictions with hostility as if they were a threat to our personal safety.

Our hostility grows in part from our sense of fustration. The forces that threaten us are beyond our personal reach. We cannot strike out and reach the Soviet Union, nor can we touch the sinister men who control the Kremlin. They leer at us from a distance, mocking our hostility. In our helpless rage against those who seek to undermine our security by hook or by crook, we strike against whatever happens to rank as a reasonable facsimile of the hated enemy. It may be a liberal college professor, a preacher who believes in brotherhood, or a lawyer who believes in justice even for those whose opinions he dislikes.

Unhappily, our hostility, bred on the altars of security, plays into the hands of the enemies of freedom. Hitler rose to power by hating and inspiring hatred for those he insisted threatened the security of the Fatherland. He grew mighty nourishing hostility toward the French, hostility toward the Jews, hostility toward the Christian church. Stalin fused his power playing on the insecurity of the Soviets, threatened by capitalist "encircle-ment." Hostility toward real or imagined enemies holds the Soviet Union together, hostility inspired by a sense of insecurity.

The third danger that falls upon us when we feel insecure is that our feelings play hob with our reason. We do not manage ourselves; we are managed by our emotions. We do not think, we feel. We do not respond to situations with intelligence; we react with emotion.

It is not easy to think clearly under the strain of insecurity and anxiety. Even in the ordinary affairs of our lives, insecurity up-sets our capacity for clear thinking. The man whose business is on solid foundations, for example, meets the strain of difficult circumstances with assurance. He knows he can weather the storm, and he meets it with confidence. But the man whose busi-ness is on the near-edge of failure meets the strain of difficult conditions under the burden of insecurity. His angers and re-sentments are close to the surface. He boils over at a drop of a hat. He thinks with his emotions instead of his mind.

The woman who feels insecure in her home, uncertain of her husband's loyalty and devotion, reacts to problems with her emotions. She can't seem to be reasonable under the circum-stances and her out-of-control emotions drive her into foolish be-havior. On the other hand, the woman who knows she is secure, surrounded by love, devotion, and trust, faces problems and difficulties with confidence. Her mind is free from the turbulence of fear, and her judgment is sound and her behavior rational.

Not long ago after I had spoken to an audience on the theme of this chapter, a young woman hurried to the platform. In broken English she said, "You took me back to my country under Hitler. I lived in Nuremburg then and I remember with terror what happened to us. It seems incredible now the way we were swept off our feet on a tide of feeling." She described a night on the street in front of the city library, the frenzy of men and women burning books, dancing and shrieking as they circled the fire. The minds of men and women were muted by the fury of their feelings.

My mind swept back to a summer in Germany. Riding on a train between Eindhoven and Cologne, I sat beside a young, educated, intelligent German. He had spent five years in Hitler's armies, fighting much of the time on the eastern front. He remembered his years as a Hitler Brown Shirt, helping to take the nation by storm. Then he remarked, "A hundred times since the war I have wondered why I did what I did. I betrayed every ideal I ever had. I violated my deepest convictions. Why? I simply was swept along with the tide."

After the inflation that left the German people feeling "harassed and helpless" in their insecurity, reason surrendered to feeling and tragedy followed. Like the luckless six hundred of the "Charge of the Light Brigade," a whole nation swept forword into the maw of unfettered feeling:

> Theirs not to reason why,
> Theirs but to do and die.[1]

Let there be no mistake, in the face of fear and insecurity, frustration and hostility, men and women all too easily surrender to the fetters of feeling, undeterred by the sanity of sound reason.

The fourth hazard follows from the other three. Insecure and anxious, we seek salvation in human personalities instead of principles. We want someone else to think for us, someone to tell us what to do and what to think. Like the Jews in their frustration before the might of Rome, we clamor for a messiah. We want a leader, strong enough and wise enough to save us. If need be, we will surrender our liberty on the altar of our security.

There is a parable of human experience in the fable of

Chicken Little, who was out in the garden one day when a cabbage leaf fell on her head. This world-shaking event filled her with terror. Quite certain that the sky was falling, she started running with all her might until she found her friend Hen Pen. The wise Hen, seeing fright in the face of Chicken Little, inquired the cause. Having been informed that the sky was falling, Hen Pen joined in the stampede. Duck Luck was next on their route, then Goose Loose, then Turkey Lurkey. In due time they all met Fox Lox. Normally they would have shunned Fox Lox like the plague, but not under the circumstances. Breathing confidence and assurance, he told them of the lovely air-raid shelter he had prepared for just such an emergency. They all ran eagerly into his den and Fox Lox lived happily ever after.

The story, of course, is quite absurd—or is it? Unhappily, it has a ring of realism in the light of recent history. The floundering of democracy in half the world has resulted when men and women, insecure and afraid, have turned from principles to personalities in search of salvation. Don't tell me it can't happen here. It can if, in our insecurity, we abandon our faith and our heritage to follow someone who assures us eloquently that he knows the way.

It is apparent, I think, that each of the four perils strikes at the heart of the faith we seek with which to manage ourselves. What is more, avoidance of the dangers depends upon our allegiance to the essentials of the Christian faith. When we are insecure and anxious, as we often seem to be, we are constrained to discover unfailing sources of inner stability with which to meet the uncertainty of our time. Indeed, there are indications that we are aware of our need for a core of faith amidst the shifting foundations of the world around us.

Somebody has described our contemporary mood as a "scramble for serenity," and that description will do as well as any other. We are scrambling for "peace of mind," "peace of soul," some way to "confident living." We want desperately to know "how to stop worrying and start living." We want inner calm while tensions are electric around us. The difficulty is that most of us want these things on our own terms, as if they could be won by self-hypnotism or something of the sort.

Once, when I announced a sermon title dealing with the problem of personal security, "The Saunterer" in the Evanston *Review* wondered if it might be well to substitute "psychiatric couches" for pews. On the contrary, I would like to substitute pews for "psychiatric couches." The simple truth is that our scramble for serenity has been mostly mental therapy with a few polite spiritual overtones. We have been trying to talk ourselves into believing in ourselves, trying to nourish our self-confidence on mental pablum sugared with pious phrases.

William James noted once that football seemed a bit like nonsense. Just see the picture: twenty-two men, bruising and battling each other for sixty minutes trying to put an oblong ball behind goal posts at the end of a field one hundred yards long. Just think of the frightful amount of energy required to accomplish a very simple objective. "Why," asked Mr. James, "doesn't somebody get up at midnight when nobody else is around and put the ball between the goal posts? It would be much simpler." The answer is obvious. The game of football demands that the ball be placed over the goal line under certain specific conditions, and without the conditions the oblong leather ball itself is altogether meaningless. So are the one-hundred-yard field and the goal lines.

Our scramble for serenity has been mostly trying to put the ball behind the goal posts at midnight. We have been trying to avoid the conditions: "Commit your way to the Lord; trust in Him."[2] Psychiatric couches are a poor substitute for spiritual commitment! They seek, too often, to avoid the conditions that lead us to inner security. We want inner security without changing our direction; peace of mind without surrender to the will of God. We want security but we also want to be free to do as we please. So, for all our mental therapy, we find ourselves just as insecure inside as the world is outside, containing no more peace inside than the world offers outside.

If we would manage our lives creatively in the face of insecurity we had best begin with the Christian faith and look for the answers to our need in the Gospels and letters that compose the New Testament. Some of the answers are summarized in the little book of I Peter, written by a man who lived in a perilous time and struggled with the problems of insecurity and violence. He said of his time that "the devil prowls around like a roaring lion, seeking someone to devour."[3] Under such circumstances, how does a man preserve his stability of mind and spirit?

Peter starts with the assumption that tough times are more or less normal. "Do not be surprised," he says, "at the fiery ordeal which comes upon you to prove you, as though something strange were happening to you."[4] There is nothing strange about insecurity and trouble. They come "as the sparks fly upward." But when they come, "Rejoice," and "glorify God" by the way you meet what you cannot avoid.

The force of Peter's argument is that Christianity is by no means a calculated pursuit of security in insecure times, but an uncalculated dedication of life to the highest in scorn of consequences. Such is the mood of the New Testament. When Herod sent word to Jesus, warning, "If you know what's good for you, you'll keep still," Jesus answered the messenger saying: "Go tell that fox . . . I must go on my way today and tomorrow and the day following,"[5] regardless of the consequences. When the leaders of the Sanhedrin ordered Peter and John to cease preaching if they knew what was good for them, they answered, "We cannot but speak of what we have seen and heard"[6] no matter what the consequences may be. Christianity is commitment to Christ without counting the cost.

When you put Christianity into the middle of everyday life where it belongs, it means integrity in business in scorn of security. In politics it means principle in scorn of votes. In the life of the church it means a quality of leadership courageous enough to reaffirm great Christian principles in scorn of criticism. In the life of a minister it means "speaking the truth in love" in scorn of comfort. In the life of a college student it means loyalty to the highest in scorn of scorn. Christianity is by no means a pious exercise in pursuit of peace of mind without reference to the practical business of living in an insecure world. It is life committed to Jesus Christ in scorn of consequences.

The strange paradox of the matter is that the deepest security any man can know comes from the great commitment of life to the lasting values that are rooted in the structure of God's universe. As Jesus put it:

Everyone . . . who hears these words of mine and does them, will be like a wise man who built his house upon the rock; and the rain fell, and the floods came, and the winds blew and beat upon that house, but it did not fall, because it was founded on the rock. And everyone who hears these words of mine and does not do them, will be like a foolish man who built his house upon the sand; and the rain fell, and the floods came and the wind blew, and beat against that house, and it fell; and great was the fall of it.[7]

You can build your life on the truths you know are true, and they will stand by you though the earth be shaken by violence or disaster.

No matter how much mental therapy he uses there is no security for the opportunist whose eye is always focused on doing what he thinks is good for him. Pilate was an opportunist. He wanted security and, no doubt, he wanted peace of mind. He wanted to keep his job, too, and to do that he had to placate his subjects. Obviously he wanted to be just to Jesus if he could manage it without risk to himself. He was, if you please, committed to his own security. That seemed quite reasonable on the face of it. Pilate was like the very comfortably fixed man who once said to me, "Well, if I don't look out for myself, who will?" He seemed quite triumphant when I confessed I had no idea who would. Six months later I thought of the answer: Pilate, the man who looked after himself! And what did he get? Not security. He even lost his job in the end. Not peace of mind. He got agony and remorse even while he was washing his hands. Not social order. He got only increasing opposition and trouble from those he tried to placate. He listened to voices threatening, "If you know what's good for you . . . ," played safe, and lost everything.

Clearly, we do not get security by playing safe and ignoring the deeper values of the human spirit. Security rests on the intangible values that sustain both our personal lives and our material civilization. It depends upon our faith in the abiding values that undergird our common life together. It rests on willingness to risk our lives in uncalculated devotion to the highest we know, no matter what the outcome.

Arthur Gossip once drew a word picture of the securest man who ever lived, marching through the years in obedience to the will of God in utter scorn of consequences. The picture began with a young man in his carpenter's shop. He was comfortable and reasonably secure. God said to him: "Are you ready?" and Jesus said: "Yes." The crowds surrounded him and then deserted him. "There's no use carrying this business of religion too far," men muttered as they went back to looking after themselves. And God said to Jesus, "Do you want to go on with it?" And Jesus said, "Yes." "He's got to be stopped," the Pharisees growled to one another. "He will destroy the *status quo*." So they hounded and hunted him to the cross. And God said: "Can you bear it for my sake and theirs?" And Jesus said, "Yes." So they nailed him to the cross and left him to die forsaken and defeated. But all the way from the carpenter shop to the cross he was the securest man who ever lived, talking about peace when his situation was not peaceful, talking about joy when circumstances around him were not joyous. "Peace I leave with you," he said. His was the security of surrender, the peace of commitment. It is the only peace there is, really.

You and I may share his peace and his strength if we dare commit our lives to him and answer his summons, "Follow thou me." We can ride through the storms of our day secure in the power of his spirit. Paul gave voice to the truth when he wrote to the Corinthians to say: "We are afflicted in every way, but not crushed; perplexed, but not driven to despair; persecuted, but not forsaken; struck down, but not destroyed."[8] And why could Paul take insecurity and peril in his stride? He had his mind fixed on Christ and on the business of building a church in his Master's name. We are "always being given up to death for Jesus' sake,"[9] he wrote, as if he could take the worst and turn it to good account.

It is futile to scramble for serenity without committing your life to something insecurity can never touch. Your own little aims can be smashed; God's aims in Christ are eternal even though they seem to be thwarted. Bonds may turn out to be worthless; but "Love never ends."[10] Bombs may blast your house to bits; but truth is everlasting. There are, as the writer of Hebrews said, some things that "cannot be shaken"[11] and remain no matter what. You can ride through the worst in scorn of consequences if your life is committed to something that will outlast it and give it meaning and worth.

That leads us to the second answer of Peter to the perils of our time. He would confront the hostility that flows from our insecurity with love and good will. "Above all things," he wrote, "hold unfailing love for one another, since love covers a multitude of sins."[12] Notice, if you will, that when life is committed to Jesus Christ, we love in scorn of consequences. Let it be noted, however, that love in the midst of hostility is not an exercise in will power; it is "the fruit of the spirit" anchored in the living God revealed in Christ.

Sometimes I am convinced that the Christian summons to love in a day of hostility is the most difficult and disturbing aspect of our faith. It is easy enough to love those who love us, but to love those who "despitefully" use us is something else. Under the stress of our insecurity and the brooding angers of our time, we are disposed to say that love and good will simply are not practical. After all, we have to be realistic.

So we come to a very basic matter. Is Christian love relevant in a world of conflict and violence? Can we afford the luxury of love and mercy, freedom and good will in the brutal and never-ending struggle for survival? In one way or another mankind has debated that question ever since what Henry Breasted called "the dawn of conscience." The question has become acute in our day because for the first time in history our conflicts and hostilities can mean ultimate self-destruction.

In his stirring play *The Firstborn,* Christopher Fry puts the question on the lips of Moses. It was by no means an academic problem, for the Hebrew people were slaves in Egypt, even as millions are slaves in our day. As Moses wrestled with the problem of how to throw off the brutal yoke of Egypt, he said:

> I need to know how good
> Can be strong enough to break out of the possessing
> Arms of evil. Where shall I look for triumph?

Then, reflectively, he added:

> Somewhere, not beyond our scope, is a power
> Participating but unharnessed, waiting
> To be led toward us. Good has a singular strength
> Not known to evil.[13]

Do we dare to believe that "Good has a singular strength not known to evil" because God Himself is in it? Will we risk "our lives, our fortunes and our sacred honor" on the faith that "good can be strong enough to break out of the possessing arms of evil" without becoming evil itself? These are moot questions as we face the political and social issues of our time. They are vital questions as we face the equally difficult personal issues of daily living.

To get down to cases, shall we love our enemies or hate them with cordial bitterness according to the modern custom? When I speak of love I do not mean a sentimental love that has no substance. I mean rather a quality of undiscourageable good will. It is what Paul meant when he wrote, not as the King James Version has it, "Love never faileth," but rather, "Love never gives up."[14] It does not get angry or lose its capacity for self-control or self-direction. It refuses to be goaded into a betrayal of its essential dignity. It is patient with the patience of God.

At the moment, we have Communist Russia on our hands, and to say "Thou shalt love" that particular enemy seems a little like inviting somebody to pat a hungry tiger on the head and say: "Nice kitty." But maybe the idea of exercising endless good will toward the Communists is not as silly as it seems. Igor Sikorsky, a Russian exile, who invented the helicopter, sensed what I mean. We were talking once about the Cold War and of developments within the Soviet Union. "You know," he said, "the only thing that sustains Soviet power is fear. I know, because I still have many contacts behind the Iron Curtain. The Russian people do not like their masters, but they have been made to believe they are encircled by enemies." He added thoughtfully, "Unfortunately our statesmen and politicians often have played into the hands of the Kremlin and helped its masters to convince the people they have grim reason to be afraid."

Then I asked him, "Tell me, is there any adequate defense against atom bombs carried by the guided missiles of our time?" He thought for a moment and then shook his head. "No," he answered, "there is no adequate military defense." Then he added, "There is no defense except good will among men and nations."

Once there was a man who believed in love and good will so much that he gave his life on a cross in their behalf, and he changed the face of the earth. He has been telling us all through the ages that it was worth what it cost because "good has a singular strength not known to evil," if we dare to believe it. With the power of God he broke out of the possessing arms of evil in the wonder of an Easter dawn. So, if Jesus Christ is an authentic revelation of God, as we Christians believe he is, we can afford to love and to exercise endless good will in scorn of consequences.

To be sure, we need to use our minds and keep our emotions under the sway of our intelligence. Peter put the matter soundly when he wrote to our condition, "gird up your minds," as if perhaps he remembered the word of his Lord, "You shall love the lord your God with all your mind."

In a time of insecurity and hostility when feeling threatens reason and we find ourselves divided against each other, we are constrained to remember two factors that go into the conclusions that determine our behavior. The first involves the facts. When we disagree it is quite possible that we arrive at our conclusions on the basis of different facts. I see one set of facts and come to one conclusion; you see another set and come to the opposite conclusion. We are somewhat like two young men who collided on the street. One young man was looking at a pretty girl and the other was window-shopping. They bumped into each other because they were looking in opposite directions.

Take such a simple matter as the weather. I look at blue skies and the bright sun as I start to work in the morning and say: "It's going to be a lovely day." You, with your rheumatism more distressing than usual, insist it is going to rain. We are looking at different facts and we arrive at opposite conclusions. You make your judgment on one set of facts and I make mine on another. Of course, the weather observer, with an abundance of facts plotted on charts and gathered from the far corners of the earth, may very well conclude that both of us are wrong. We will have neither sunshine nor rain, but fog. Our judgments are decisively colored by the particular set of facts we examine.

Obviously, the Christian mind, seeking sound conclusions in a time of hostility and conflict, will pursue all the relevant facts in any situation. Sanity demands willingness to look unblinkingly at all the facts, whether they support our feelings or not.

There is a suggestion of the spirit of the sound mind in the behavior of a test pilot who lost his life during the early days of the Second World War. While he was testing a new four-engine plane it began to disintegrate under the strain of violent maneuvers. Six of the seven-man crew parachuted to safety, but the pilot stayed at his post radioing a precise record of what was happening to the plane to those on the ground. When it was too late to jump, he called, "Sorry," over the radio and crashed. His comrades had the following legend inscribed on his tombstone: "He died to get the facts."

Facts are essential to sound judgment, but they are by no means the whole story. You would think that when we both examine the same facts we would arrive at identical conclusions. Unhappily, that is not the case. There is a second reason for our disagreements and our hostility toward each other: the particular point of view from which we look at the facts. There is an episode in S. N. Behrman's *The Talley Method* which goes far toward revealing the source of our hostilities. Enid, a delightful and discerning young woman, refuses to marry Dr. Talley, whose standards and ideals are quite different from her own. Surprised and angered, he says: "You're not going to let a difference in point of view separate us?"[15] She answers, "But that's all that ever does separate people." Her insight is profoundly true. Our different points of view lead us to different conclusions even when we wrestle with the same essential facts.

The airing of differences between civilian executives of the Army and Senator Joseph McCarthy in the spring of 1954 strikingly shows that not facts but points of view determine the nature of our thinking. The millions who watched the affair on television all witnessed the same people giving the same testimony. However, the conclusions of those who watched were altogether different. They were dictated by the feelings of people, feelings that represented their particular points of view. There were those whose fears led them to the conclusion that subversives must be rooted out of government no matter what the methods involved and even though the innocent may be hurt. There were others who looked upon the spectacle feeling deeply that basic democratic and Christian principles must be preserved while we are in the process of eliminating Communists. The two groups came to opposite conclusions on the basis of the same essential facts.

The difficulty is that we suffer from what might be called emotional blind spots when our feelings run high. I may be charged with a yellow idea that represents security to me. You may be rational, intelligent, and sustained by the facts as you come to me preaching a blue idea. But either of two things happens in all probability. I cling tenaciously to my yellow idea, blind to logic under the stress of my emotions, or possibly a very small measure of your reason breaks through. However, I do not get the blue idea, with all its soundness and rationality. I get a green idea, a bit of the blue of reason mixed with a strong measure of emotional yellow.

When we find ourselves in situations of conflict and emotional tension there are, therefore, two questions we need to ask: The first is: What are the facts that are relevant to the issue; have I looked at all the facts? And second: From what point of view am I examining the facts? The importance of the questions is suggested in the behavior of a woman who went to a high-school superintendent during the discussion concerning the Bricker Amendment to the Constitution, which would have limited the powers of the President in international negotiation. "When my children come home from high school," she complained, "I have to unteach them." To which the superintendent replied: "But we try to present both sides of issues as carefully as possible." "That's what I mean," the woman answered. "There's only one correct side to the question."

That is a striking illustration of an emotional reaction to insecurity. It issued first in a refusal to look at all the facts and second in a refusal to admit there could be more than one possible vantage point from which to view the facts. Behavior emerging from any such process is more likely to be wrong than right.

The important matter is to recognize that we bring our points of view, our prejudices, our feelings, our fears, and our hurts to bear on the problems of an insecure time, and our behavior is motivated more by our emotions than by our reason, unless we are keenly aware that our feelings are deeply involved. Even in little things, like our judgment of people, our thinking is colored by our point of view. An unknown poet put the matter with whimsical humor. A child was disturbed by her mother's antagonism toward the garbage man, and she remarked:

> We have the nicest garbage man,
> He empties out our garbage can;
> He's just as nice as he can be.
> He always stops and talks with me.
> My mother doesn't like his smell,
> But then, she doesn't know him well.[16]

Our thinking about the garbage man will be guided by whether we are concerned with the unpleasant nature of a particular work a man does or whether we "know him well" enough to discover that really "He's just as nice as he can be."

There are, then, two basic concerns of the Christian girding his mind for a time of insecurity. The first is the facts. The second is the resolution to see the facts from the point of view of the mind of Christ. It makes no difference whether we are dealing with the garbage man or the question of segregation. We can look at the garbage man with condescension and avoid him because he smells, or we can accept him as a man because he is a child of God, and underneath "he's nice." We can look at the question of segregation from the point of view of our conviction that white people are superior; or we can view it from the heights of our devotion to the mind of Christ.

Plainly we need to look at the issues of an insecure time stabilized mentally and emotionally by our abiding devotion to the lasting values of our human heritage as they are revealed in the mind of Christ. Are we acting in obedience to our faith in freedom under God? Does our thinking square with our belief in the sacredness of human personality? Does it keep faith with justice and rule by law which can be applied in every situation and to all men? Is it motivated by undiscourageable good will?

We cannot afford what has been called "crisis behavior,"

which acts in response to feeling undeterred by reason marching in obedience to facts interpreted in loyalty to the mind of Christ. Peter's admonition is altogether relevant to our situation: "Gird up your minds."[17]

That brings us to the final word of Peter to a time of insecurity and peril when we are in danger of following messiahs in search of safety. Says Peter, "Cast your anxieties on him [God], for he cares about you."[18] That affirmation is the very heart of the Christian faith: "He cares about you"—you personally and individually.

Obviously, the love of God does not save us from the hurts of our common life. The symbol of the Christian faith is a cross, not a bed of roses. There may be times when the tides roll over us and we feel as impotent as King Canute, ordering the waters to cease encroaching on his domain. God does not compel the waves to cease their flowing, but He gives us grace to breast them and to survive, still strong. His love is revealed, not in the absence of cross-crowned Calvaries, but in strength to meet and use them for His Kingdom's sake.

The haunting lines of the little song from Maxwell Anderson and Kurt Weill's play version of *Cry, the Beloved Country* put the truth in a way that is unforgettable:

> Before Lord God made the sea and the land
> He held all the stars in the palm of his hand,
> And they ran through his fingers like grains of sand,
> And one little star fell alone.

> Then the Lord God hunted through the wide night air
> For the little dark star on the wind down there—
> And he stated and promised he'd taken special care
> So it wouldn't get lost again.

> Now a man don't mind if the stars grow dim
> And the clouds blow over and darken him,
> So long as the Lord God's watching over them,
> Keeping track how it all goes on.

But I've been walking through the night and the day
Till my eyes get weary and my head turns gray,
And sometimes it seems maybe God's gone away,
Forgetting the promise that we heard him say—
And we're lost out there in the stars.

Little stars, big stars
Blowing through the night,
And we're lost out here in the stars.[19]

Well, maybe we feel lost, insecure, and anxious, "blowing through the night," but we never really are lost, for God's love never lets go. It is as steady as the stars and patient beyond anything we know of patience. It is our refuge and our strength, the final security of the soul in a time of insecurity and hostility, rampant emotions and searching for messiahs. In the love and strength of God, "good can be strong enough" in our time "to break out of the possessing arms of evil," and by faith we can manage our lives to that end.

CHAPTER VIII

You Can Worry Wisely

YOU worry because you are afraid of something. Maybe you are afraid your sins will find you out, or possibly you are fearful lest something unpleasant happen to you, or you are troubled lest your plans go awry. You can find plenty of things to be anxious about in any average lifetime—your business, your health, your children. If you put your mind to it and let it run, you can have a nervous breakdown just from worrying about one thing or another. You can develop insomnia, ulcers, heart trouble, and headache by the simple process of keeping yourself in good supply of matters that worry you.

You can think about your problems or you can worry about them, and there is a vast difference between the two. Worry is thinking that has turned toxic. It is jarring music that goes round and round and never comes to either climax or conclusion. Thinking works its way through problems to conclusions and decisions; worry leaves you in a state of tensely suspended animation. When you worry, you go over the same ground endlessly and come out the same place you started. Thinking makes progress from one place to another; worry remains static. The problem of life is to change worry into thinking and anxiety into creative action.

Fear is not altogether a misfortune unless it ends in the
paralysis of perpetual anxiety. Some years ago I nearly stepped
on a rattlesnake, basking in the sun. I am sure I jumped at
least ten feet. My fear gave me wings, and I was deeply grateful. No doubt your fear of the Collector of Internal Revenue
helps to keep you from tax troubles with Uncle Sam. We warn
our children that it is dangerous to play with matches. We give
them a healthy fear of fire when they are small. But we do not
want them to live in permanent anxiety, worried by fire even
when it is in the furnace. Not all fears are groundless by any
means, but fears that turn into habitual anxiety are altogether
foolish. I am afraid to put my hand on a hot stove, but I do
not go around constantly anxious lest I accidentally touch something hot. My fear of touching a hot stove is mitigated by my
intelligence.

Whenever you are afraid, you may be sure that life is trying
to teach you something. Your fears are an invitation both to
learn and to think. Your fear of smallpox is an invitation to
consider the possibility of having yourself vaccinated. Your
concern for your health should lead you to a sane manner of
living. Your fear of ignorance is a challenge to be informed.
If you are disturbed about your children, that is simply an open
invitation to study child psychology, to discover why they behave
the way they do, and perhaps to reorganize your own life if they
have developed an allergy to you. Every fear is a challenge to
discovery and insight.

So your fears, anxieties, and worries can be your friends if
you recognize them as opportunities for insight and understanding. Your fears are a hazard and a peril if you let them turn
toxic so that they poison your whole life. Obviously it is important at the outset to get your worries out into the open in
order to see them objectively. You will discover on analysis
that some of them are altogether irrational and futile, while

others have a sound basis in fact. Separate the sheep from the
goats. See your silly worries as absurd and then put your mind
and your faith to work on the others. Usually you can manage
justified worries if they are not complicated by a clutter of unwarranted anxieties.

When we look into our minds it is clear that imagination
supplies an astonishing number of irrational worries. Imagination, said Smitty in the comic strip, is "seein' movin' pictures
with your eyes shut." That definition will do as well as any
other and better than most. Most of us see too many moving
pictures with our eyes shut. We see ourselves crossing perilous
bridges, trying futilely to meet impossible situations and to
manage incredible circumstances we probably never will confront. At luncheon a bank president described his experience
with a bit of whimsical capacity to laugh at himself. "I got to
feeling a bit under par," he said, "and I was sure I had an
ulcer. I worried about it until I really got sick. So I went to the
hospital. The doctors gave me tests and took X-rays. After
some anxious waiting I got their report. They could not find
anything wrong with me and no signs of an ulcer. Believe it or
not, the next day I felt better."

We can imagine all manner of ills to keep us anxious and
worried. Charles T. Holman observes that most of us are like
a businessman who went to a psychiatrist.[1] He was a bundle
of nerves and worries. The psychiatrist asked him to make a list
of his worries and it turned out that 40 per cent of them centered in things that were not likely to happen. The man still had
60 per cent of his worries left, but at least he cut his load nearly
in half when he learned to laugh at the imaginary 40 per cent.

When I was a small boy my father always worried for fear
I would tumble off the woodshed at our summer home. Perversely, I would rather be on that woodshed than anywhere
else. Then my boys came along, and my father took up his

worrying where he left it when I grew to the age of discretion. My boys were as perverse about the woodshed as I had been. They seemed to love perilous perches. One day when my father was watching two of my boys sitting on the woodshed's highest point, he turned to me and remarked: "For forty years I have been worrying for fear somebody would fall off that woodshed and nobody ever has."

During a polio epidemic in a midwestern city a doctor was talking about polio. He has two children, and said he, "I know that not one child in a million will have polio. I know from my own practice that there are relatively few deaths from polio, and most of those who have it recover. I know all that and I tell my wife it is silly to worry about polio. I tell my patients the same thing over and over. Then I go home and worry for fear my children will get polio." So we see moving pictures of disaster with our eyes shut and grow old and neurotic worrying about things that probably will not happen. In one way or another we are like the kindly old gentleman who spent thirty years of his life afraid the company he worked for would fail. There were, to be sure, some bad days during the depression when the company had difficult going. They only added fuel to the old man's fears. He fretted and fussed and wondered what on earth he would do. He had given the best years of his life to the company and he could not bear the thought of having to start over. He died some time ago and the company is still going strong. He wasted his nervous strength and dissipated his powers seeing frightening moving pictures with his eyes shut.

A Boston newspaper used to carry these lines at the top of its editorial column:

> Some of your hurts, you have cured
> And the sharpest you still have survived;
> But what torments of grief you've endured
> From the evils that never arrived.

Get your imaginary fears out into the open and have a good laugh at yourself. You can cut your worry load nearly in half and find a new lift for living.

When the businessman Charles Holman described had catalogued the worries that were mostly in his imagination and were not likely to happen, he looked at his remaining anxieties and discovered that to the 40 per cent in his imagination he could add 30 per cent of his worries as things that already had happened and could not be changed.

One of the hardest things most of us have to learn is to make decisions and then stop second-guessing. You buy a dress and then worry all night wondering if you made the right choice. You decide to be chairman of the welcome committee and then spend a week worrying whether you should have accepted the appointment. You have a party and then worry for weeks because you did not invite somebody you think maybe you should have included. You say something somewhere and then spend a sleepless night wishing you had not said it. I know a businessman who sold his business ten years ago and he is still worrying over whether he did the right thing.

You cannot change what has already happened. What is done is done. If what you did was morally wrong, you can set about the business of making retribution and being forgiven; but if what you did was a matter of judgment without moral factors, worry won't do a thing except give you nervous indigestion. There was a bit of somber wisdom in William Gladstone, who was walking one day with a friend. They went through a pasture gate, and the friend, who came through last, neglected to close the gate. Gladstone turned, closed the gate, and remarked: "I have made it a habit all through life to close gates behind me."

You have to close the gates on yesterday or today will be miserable. Close the gate on your failures. There is no use worrying about them, wishing you had been wiser than you were. The brooding memory of a marriage that failed marked Mary, Queen of Scots, for failure. She could not close the gate and press on. You made a careless mistake. You should not have made it but you did, and you have been nervous and upset about it. If you don't stop worrying you will make more mistakes. Close the gate and push on. You missed a chance to make a sale because you were careless or overconfident. There is no use worrying now. You learned a lesson. Close the gate now and keep on going. You lost patience with your children and said things you wish you had left unsaid. You have been troubled about your lack of self-control. Maybe you need to say, "I'm sorry," then close the gate and make the best of today. You cannot change yesterday. You can be rid of 30 per cent of your worries if you will put yesterday behind you and keep your mind on today with its possibilities. Put your hand to the plow and look forward, not backward.

The businessman's catalogue assigned his worries 40 per cent to imagination and 30 per cent to what could not be changed. He still had 30 per cent left. Twelve per cent he came to see centered around what other people would say or think. Like all of us, he wanted social approval the worst way. He wanted a cheering section that would not do any booing. So he did not wish to make any misplays that would bring on disapproval.

You know as well as I that we carry a cargo of misery when we are perpetually worried over what somebody else will think of what we do or say. Unhappily, we get into the habit of resting our worth on the judgment of other people. Approval, congratulations, and flattery become the crutches upon which we limp through life and we fall on our faces if somebody kicks a crutch out from under us with a bit of criticism. The result is that we are forever worried for fear something we do will bring disapproval upon us.

A woman will buy a new hat and if nobody happens to notice

it she will worry for fear it isn't becoming. We spend more than we can afford to win approval by our apparent affluence and then worry about the bills. We will not say what we honestly think because the crowd seems to think otherwise, and then we worry because we went along. My oldest son used to wear jeans to school. He said everybody else wore them. Furthermore, he wore them about as far down on his hips as they would go and still stay on. He insisted all the boys wore them that way. It would be a crime to be different! Once his mother remarked: "But what will people think of us when they see him dressed that way?" I don't know, but I am inclined to think they did not notice; at least I hope not.

"The animals are happy," Voltaire once said. "They don't know what people say about them."[2] We know, or at least we suspect. Even the greatest of men are sensitive to what other people say, or perhaps it would be more accurate to say they are sensitive to what they think other people are saying or thinking about them. They may be altogether wrong, and in any case they cannot manage their lives to suit other people. I am inclined to think that most people say and think far less about our affairs than we imagine.

In any case, the habit of worrying about what others think of us is quite devastating. It robs us of our independence and crowds us into a mold until we are disposed to think what the crowd thinks and to let the opinions of our social set become our opinions. We act the way our group acts, conforming to the accepted behavior patterns around us. To be out of step is unthinkable. To challenge the thinking of our class is outside the possible. We would rather be wrong with those whose approval we wish than right and out of step. It is a sin to be different when we are forever worried about what others will think of what we say or do!

We want to be free, and yet we surrender our freedom on the

altar of our anxiety to conform, to avoid criticism. Basically, the threat to our freedom comes not from the power of a state to coerce but from our inward fear of being out of step. We surrender our freedom through our will to conform long before external power takes that freedom from us. It is the prophets who dare to challenge the axioms of society who preserve our freedom for us. It is the thinkers who anchor their lives to first principles and become "his majesty's loyal opposition" who undergird our liberty. What other people think is by no means a sound criterion for human behavior, and to worry over criticism is the first step toward the surrender of independence.

You have your own life to live. What other people think is beside the point. You do not need to be deliberately offensive or belligerent and certainly not opinionated and unwilling to consider the convictions of others. Take your stand on first principles and dare to be "off the reservation" of crowd opinion and behavior if need be, and don't torment yourself about what somebody else thinks. You can get rid of a sizable section of your worries that way.

There is another area of worry that composes 10 per cent of your total worry load. It concerns your health. To be sure, health is a major concern of life and you want to be healthy. You have an obligation to be as healthy and well as sane living can keep you. Elementary good sense requires a decent concern for health. But to be constantly worried for fear you will have a stroke, get cancer, or die of heart failure is the essence of folly. Worry is the surest way there is to ill health, for the mind and the body are intimately interlinked. Each works on the other for good or for ill.

You know full well that you can "worry yourself sick." A friend of mine who spent most of his time fretting about his health went to the hospital for a rather simple operation. He refused to believe his illness was not serious. He feared he would not pull through. The doctors assured him there was no cause for alarm. As the hour for the operation approached, my friend was literally frantic with fear. He died a few hours after the operation. Two doctors said bluntly that he was simply "scared to death." He did not need to die. Literally, he worried himself to death.

That brings us to the final 8 per cent of our worries that are legitimate. Here we face those areas of concern we cannot write off as absurd. They are real and they demand attention. We cannot ignore them, deny their reality, or escape from them. They have to be faced honestly and soberly, but they can be met creatively and decisively. When we meet them, however, it is important first of all to cut them down to size. As a Canadian soldier wrote to his father: "Dad, the difficulties of life decrease the moment they are faced." It is so.

There is a suggestive story of Miobi, the boy who lived "far to the South beyond the Third Cataract"[3]—how he went on a journey to overcome his fears. The story is told with great charm by Ralph Lavers, and it is in a collection called *The Scarlet Fish and Other Stories*. Miobi had come to a village where the people were doing nothing but moan and wail. The fires were not lit, the goats were not milked because all the villagers were expecting to be eaten shortly by the monster on the top of the mountain. This monster had the head of a crocodile and the body of a hippopotamus and a tail like a very fat snake, and smoke came from his fiery breath. But Miobi said, "I will go up the mountain and challenge the monster."

There he was, sure enough, but as the boy climbed and came nearer, the monster looked definitely smaller. "This is very curious indeed," he said. "The further I am away from the monster, the larger it seems, and the nearer I am to it, the smaller it seems." When the boy reached the cave, he found no monster but a quiet little thing as small as a frog, which purred, and he brought it home as a pet.

Such was the experience of a friend who looked misfortune in the face during the depression and cut it down to a size he could manage. He lost his money. Then he lost his job. He thought for a while he could not stand it, but after the first shock he moved from Chicago to a forlorn little farm in Missouri, into which he put the last cent he had. The house was dilapidated and had no conveniences. Much of the land was eroded. But he and his wife faced their bad luck and decided to make the best of it. Now, on their little farm they do not have much, but you would not know the place, and they are happier than they have ever been. They would not trade their farm for Chicago and New York thrown into the bargain. Their monster diminished when they met it face to face and turned it into a friend.

Most of the problems that worry us can be cut down to manageable proportions when we face them unblinkingly. Even though worse comes to worst everything is not lost; the worst that can happen can be trimmed to size and managed. So a woman of sixty-five discovered when her husband, a Missouri farmer, died quite suddenly, leaving her nothing for the future. She might have lived with her children and complained of the fates that made her dependent. But she did nothing of the sort. The problem was clear enough, from her point of view. At sixty-five, what could she do to support herself? Obviously, there were many things she could not do. She put her mind to work on her problem, and shortly she had the answer.

One year prior to her husband's death she had spent a month in a hospital as a patient. She remembered the food. It had been poorly prepared. She knew she could cook. Indeed, she was an expert. So, saying nothing to her children, she went to the hospital, got a job in the kitchen, and remained on the job until she died at seventy-two. She cut her problem down to a size she could manage and meet with the talent she possessed, and she marched through the years with her head high and with a feeling of meaningful achievement.

A wise banker coined a helpful slogan for those worried by their debts: "Put all your debts in one basket. We'll hold the basket while you empty it month by month." While the banker is doing very well for himself, he says he has a sense of mission too. He hates to see people worried half-sick by their bills. "You'd be surprised," he remarked, "how relieved people are when they see a way to manage their debts. They are grateful when we help them plan a budget that they can handle while they are paying their obligation to us."

Whether you are worried about your debts, your future, or anything else, you can cut your worry down to manageable proportions and deal with it if you will. What is of decisive importance is the fact that when your problems turn out to be manageable they cease to worry you. You feel a profound sense of relief, and more, you find satisfaction in achievement and conquest.

Having whittled your problem down to size, consider what resources you can bring to bear to meet it. There is no situation so grim as to be impossible of resolution. We always possess resources we have not yet discovered, and often they are decisive.

One vital resource is the simple but eloquent affirmation: "I can manage." Prospects may seem "black as the pit from pole to pole," but what comes out of the darkness hinges largely on whether we say "I can" or "I can't." To say "I can't" when clouds are heavy over our days is to cultivate the anxious fears that leave us feeble for the testing time to come. To say "I can" is to rally the powers of the spirit for a grim attack on the situation looming on the horizon. Many a man has lost a glowing chance for victory over himself and events by approaching crises negatively and so failing to gather his own strength for the contest.

George Sisler, Brooklyn Dodger scout, who twice hit over .400 in the American League, cites three musts for young men who want to play baseball, and they are suggestive for us as we face the problems that trouble us. First, "The hitter must be unafraid at the plate . . . because fear makes weak curve-ball hitters." So a man who expects to hit starts necessarily with the firm belief: "I can." Second, "Don't think about taking a pitch . . . be prepared to hit everything that comes up and, if it's bad, lay off." In short, don't just take the worst that comes along without challenging it. If there is a chance for a hit, swing; if not, bide your time and await an opportunity. Third, "Expect every pitch to be a fast ball . . . then, if it's a curve, you have time to adjust your swing." Get set for what's coming in the faith that you can manage whatever it is, a fast ball or a curve.

Batting in the big leagues is no different from batting against odds in life. The approach has to be positive, one of confidence, or we go down without getting the bat from our shoulders. We may strike out, confidence or no confidence, but the .300 hitters are men who believe they can hit. So in life, the men and women who take life's fast balls and curves in their stride and get on base against odds are those who face their days saying to themselves, "I can manage."

When storm clouds gather and our souls are shaken by "the shape of things to come" for us, the words "I can't" betoken failure and defeat—without a struggle. To be sure, we may go down under the blows we face even when we say "I can," but we need not stay down. It may well be that when the smoke has cleared we shall have "but half of a broken dream for a pillow

at night," but if we know we can take the worst and keep
going we can. We need not grovel in the dust with a whimper.
We can rise again with a shout.

It isn't the winning that matters, but the heart to keep plowing on. It may be that we shall of necessity recast our expectations, but we can manage if we know we can. There is a hint
of the mood of the victors in the lines of John G. Neihardt:

> More than half-beaten, but fearless,
> Facing the storm and the night;
> Breathless and reeling but tearless,
> Here in the lull of the fight,
> I who bow not but before thee,
> God of the fighting Clan,
> Lifting my fists, I implore Thee,
> Give me the heart of a man.[4]

There is no time for worry when we set our faces steadfastly
toward our Jerusalems to meet our crosses, believing we can
manage them when and if they come. When we are still pushing
on "More than half-beaten, but fearless," we rally the resources
of our own spirits that bear us onward.

Worry is a token of our negativism, of our failure to affirm,
"I can" in the face of uninviting situations. Courage is the
evidence of the affirmative mood of the soul whose powers have
been rallied and united.

There is another resource to be found: in the comradeship of
others who believe in us. The testing times that loom before
us are assuaged and worries overcome by the faith of those who
believe in us, even when we are on the verge of losing faith
in ourselves. I felt the truth once while being driven over a
twisting mountain road. We came to a tortuous, rocky hill, and
the woman who was driving stopped the car and looked fearfully ahead. "Do you think I can drive up there?" she asked
her husband. "Of course you can," he answered. We bounced

our way to the crest of the hill and her husband, smiling broadly, said: "I knew you could do it."

What a priceless resource there is for troubled lives in the comradeship of those who encourage us to believe in ourselves. Who can measure what it meant to Timothy, anxious and troubled as he began to preach, when word came from Paul saying: "O Timothy, stir up the gift that is in thee." Poor Timothy, fighting against odds, had well-nigh forgotten the gift and the resources of his mind and spirit. The fact that Paul, his good friend, believed in him was a source of courage to go on. So Barnabas, lending his strength to John Mark, brought greatness out of what had been anxiety and cowardice.

In a thousand ways we borrow faith and hope for worried days from those whose belief in us is strong. Even a child can sense the meaning of a borrowed confidence. The truth came home to me long years ago when I left a hospital room where a child lay grievously ill. Her mother walked with me down the corridor. "You know," she said, "when I went into Mary's room this afternoon I asked her how she felt. She answered, 'Let me look at you, mother.' I turned and smiled and she said: 'I'm feeling better today, mother. I always can tell how I am by the way you look.' "

How often that is true. Anxiety is catching, like a cold, and so is faith. Now and then when worries bear us down and our faith in ourselves is at low ebb there is a sturdy resource in fellowship with those who still believe in us. As someone said of another: "There were times when I carried on just because I believed in his belief in me." Who has not shared that experience in testing hours when lights burned low and hopes were dim?

The strength and courage of the men and women who began the Christian Church were buttressed by the faith of others. Their days were often anxious ones while persecution fell upon them. The luckless perished to entertain the mobs who swarmed the circus, or died on burning crosses, turning night to day. But, believing in each other, they sustained each other. They believed in themselves because the comradeship believed in them. They had something to be worried about, but they did not worry.

A corollary resource for anxious days is in the knowledge that others are depending on us to be strong. A G.I. who spent eighteen months in Korea, not knowing if he ever would be home again, found other men looking to him in their fear. "It was a novel experience," he said, "but the feeling others were depending on me kept me steady when hunger and filth and brutality made me wonder why go on." His words give point to Paul's observation: "Bear ye one another's burdens." Paradoxically, we find strength to bear our own troubles and worries when we are bearing the burdens of others who are depending on us.

One striking technique devised by Alcoholics Anonymous helps to reinforce the notion that the fact of others leaning on us is a resource. The alcoholic, struggling against the tides of the past, goes through the days fearful lest he slip again. So he is admonished to assume responsibility for another alcoholic. You would think the added burden of responsibility for another would double anxiety and worry. On the contrary, it divides the strain. As one old-timer in Alcoholics Anonymous noted, "With half a dozen of the boys depending on me, I haven't time to worry about myself." Then he added reflectively, "While I am giving them a hand I don't have to worry about myself."

Maybe our courage in testing circumstances is half pretense when we know others are depending on us, but there is a resource even when we lend pretended strength. One boy put the truth simply when he and a companion were lost for several days in the Colorado Rockies. "I was scared stiff, but Bill was calm as anything, so I kept going." And Bill replied, "I was scared stiff too, but I couldn't let Bob know how I felt, so I kept going." The sense of dependence was a mutual resource. We are somewhat like a bridge threatened by a flood. We need to be weighted down. When pounding waters threaten a railroad bridge, engines and heavily loaded cars are run onto the bridge. The more weight it carries, the more pounding it endures. It is so in life. The heavier our responsibility is for others who depend on us, the more shocks we can endure without foundering. Those who depend upon us are a mighty resource when the clouds are dark around us and we are threatened by our fears.

Happily, we need not stand in human strength alone, and there is a source of courage from beyond ourselves. It is well, for there are times of strain beyond our strength, as a young man understood after listening to Kipling's lines:

> If you can keep your head when all about you
> Are losing theirs and blaming it on you,
> If you can trust yourself when all men doubt you,
> But make allowance for their doubting too;
> If you can wait and not be tired by waiting,
> Or being lied about, don't deal in lies,
> Or being hated don't give way to hating,
> And yet don't look too good, nor talk too wise
> . . . .
> Yours is the Earth and everything that's in it,
> And, which is more—you'll be a man my son.[5]

"But," asked the young man, "what if you can't?" And that, of course, is the deepest question and it drives us beyond the resources on the human level to that which lies beyond in God.

There is weather wisdom for us all in the behavior of the Apostle Paul, who worried for a while over his "thorn in the flesh." We do not know precisely what it was—malaria, epilepsy, eye disease, or something else; scholars are not agreed. In any case, Paul was anxious. He tells us he prayed over the matter, asking God to take away his affliction. But Paul went on suffering to the end of his days. A lesser man would have said it was not fair and perhaps retreated into the lassitude of ill health. But not Paul. He accepted it as something to be endured and used by the grace of God. Said he, "I will all the more gladly boast of my weaknesses, that the power of Christ may rest upon me."[6]

If we accept the disturbing possibilities that worry and fret us and seek the resources of God, even the most shattering experience can be creative. G. Studdert-Kennedy found it so. He was a great British poet and preacher who struggled along against the ravages of tuberculosis. But he gave up worrying about it when he finally took Paul's words seriously. "I can do all things in him who strengtheneth me."[7] Quite literally he did. I heard him speak once years ago at a Student Volunteer Convention at Indianapolis. He looked like a shadow when he shuffled to the stage to speak to seven thousand students who were gathered there. Plainly, he had taken the worst that life could do and used it to demonstrate "the power of Christ" to carry him through. He, more than any other, stirred that crowd of students.

Never discount the resource of faith in "the power of Christ." Passing through one of the most difficult times of his life, with his career in the balance, William James noted in one of his letters home that he was by no means fearful. He added, then, that "My appeal is to nothing more difficult than religious faith." So, living by faith, he faced the worst without the fear of failure. As Walt Whitman put it, "Faith is the antiseptic of the soul"; it disinfects the fears which make us long for some "honorable discharge from the bankrupt business of living."

Living by faith is like going to sea in a seaworthy ship you know will not sink in a storm; living fearfully is like going to sea in a sieve. Whether you go to sea in a sound ship or in a sieve, you know very well you will run into storms. You will meet foul weather as well as fair. The difference lies in the fact that when you are in a sound bottom you know you can manage the storm. You do not need to be afraid. Faith is simply trust, in scorn of storms. It is the inner knowledge that with God we are seaworthy and do not need to be anxious.

It should be observed, however, that the resource of faith in "the power of Christ" is not something we pull out of thin air in an emergency. It is a habit of mind born in spiritual discipline. Recently, for example, I played my annual game of golf with the results about what you would expect. After several of my shots had landed in water or gotten lost in trees, it occurred to me that I was approaching golf fearfully rather than confidently. So with perfect faith I addressed my next drive. It turned out to be a fifty-foot putt. Then I realized that faith rested not on an act of resolute will but upon experience. As John said, "Perfect love casts out fear."[8] The only way I could approach my shots confidently and with faith would be for me to love golf enough to be disciplined by it. I would have to play golf two or three times a week, master its techniques and timing, and achieve the skills golf demands.

We get to the point of living by faith in "the power of Christ" through practice. "Perfect love casts out fear" and leads us to accept spiritual disciplines. When we love God enough to seek His will and to do it day by day, we can face our hazards with faith and confidence. What is more, when we face a real problem with faith in God, the problem does not look the same as when we look at it fearfully. There were plenty of men who had faced Goliath, the Philistine giant, fearfully. Saul's whole army was afraid. When Goliath filled the valley with his mocking laughter, Saul's men were ready to give up the fight. When David faced Goliath with confidence in God, it did not occur to him to be afraid. Not even Goliath could put God to rout. David knew that from long experience. When the Christians of the first century were surrounded by opposition and hounded by persecution, they seem to have been fearless. The author of the Book of Romans set the temper of their mood when he said: "If God be for us, who is against us?"[9] They faced their hazards in faith and went on to conquer the world.

Confront two businessmen with precisely the same problem. One of them will meet it fearfully. He cannot eat and he cannot sleep. He becomes jittery, irritable, and inefficient. He cannot think clearly; he makes mistakes that complicate his problem. He is desperately afraid he will do the wrong thing. In all probability he will exercise poor judgment and his forebodings will be fulfilled. The other man faces his problem in faith. He knows the issues are critical. Everything depends upon clear thinking and sound judgment. Nevertheless, he sleeps well. He awakens refreshed to survey the possibilities quietly. He draws heavily upon his spiritual resources for serenity and poise. He is altogether certain that with God at the helm of his life he can do what must be done to see the issue through wisely. He comes through his struggle stronger than he was.

Two people face similar illnesses. From a medical point of view their chances of survival are equal. But one of them goes into the illness fearfully. He is tense and anxious. He tries to manage his own case. He feels no confidence in anybody and he doubts he has much chance to get well. His fears hinder the healing process and complicate his illness. His mind plays havoc with his body and his recovery is retarded or defeated. The other man meets his illness sure of the strength of God. He is relaxed in mind and in spirit, undergirded by his faith in the Everlasting Arms. His serenity is an impetus to his healing. As

Isaiah put it, "In quietness and in trust shall be your strength."[10] When a man is living by faith, he meets the hazards of his life prayerfully and finds lifting power. George Meredith describes the lifting power of confident prayer in the words of Dr. Shrapnel, one of his characters. "And take this for the good in prayer," says the good doctor, "that it makes us repose on the unknown with confidence, makes us flexible to change, makes us ready for revolution—for life—then! He who has the fountain of prayer in him will not complain of hazards. Cast forth the soul in prayer, you meet the creative elements giving breath to you."[11]

That leads us to the final resource that stems from the mind of Christ. It is the certainty that no matter what happens there is solid ground on which to stand. Paul understood the matter when his world was tumbling around his ears. "The things that are seen are transient," he wrote, "but the things that are unseen are eternal."[12] Behind the façade on the surface of life there were deeps of reality that would not fail. Men could build their lives on the transient, forgetting the forever and the values that last if they wished. Caiaphas did, and Pilate and Herod. But there is neither stability nor courage in the transient.

You and I need to learn what Caiaphas and Pilate and Herod did not learn until it was too late. They indulged in what somebody called "crisis behavior," with nothing of the forever in it. But events betrayed them because a crisis in personal affairs makes no difference whatever in the eternal values that both judge and sustain our lives. In truth,

> . . . the slow watches of the night
> Not less belong to God.

There is courage and there is stability for us in the midst of events that trouble us if we know that the transient episodes of our lives come and go against a background of the unseen and the eternal. Television provides a suggestive analogy, for every transient program you see on the television screen comes to you by virtue of a background that holds together and yet is unseen. You watch the Cisco Kid riding the range, or you see Arthur Godfrey drinking tea. But in the background are the unseen forces of the universe, mysterious and unfathomable, that enable you to see pictures on a screen in your living room. In all probability your television gets out of adjustment now and then, and you cannot see anything but meaningless blotches. When that happens, you do not blame the unseen forces of the universe. You assume that something is wrong inside the contraption in your living room. The unseen is forever dependable, and either you adjust your television receiver to it or you get nothing but a bad temper. In a very real sense you have to say to the unseen forces that make television possible, "Not my will, but thine be done."[13]

So Jesus understood that there are unseen spiritual forces in the universe to which all men must say, "Not my will, but thine be done." Complain all you please in anxious days that life is

> . . . a tale told by an idiot,
> Full of sound and fury,
> Signifying nothing.[14]

but you may rest assured that the trouble is in you, not in life. Argue if you wish that "life is simply a long headache on a noisy street," but you may be certain that in one way or another you are living at cross purposes with the forces of forever. You are in conflict with the Eternal and it is too big for you. You cannot possibly conduct a successful campaign against it; nobody can. I would like to say that to the present Soviet leader as Lafayette said it to Napoleon. I would like to say it to political leaders as Lincoln said it to Stephen Douglas. I would like to say it to you as Jesus said it on his cross. Neither men nor nations can stand against the tides of forever. So Paul understood when he wrote: "We never lose heart . . . because we look not to the things that are seen, but to the things that are unseen; for the things that are seen are transient, but the things that are unseen are eternal."[15]

Through the last days of Holy Week, Caiaphas obviously was very real, and his power to condemn Jesus was plain to anyone. On secular terms, Jesus should have been worried. He was not. The immutable truth, running through the fabric of the universe, was something no man could see. Nevertheless, Jesus knew it was there. It was, in one sense, like the water in a swimming pool, sustaining those who trust it and sinking those who fight it in mistrust. Caiaphas fought it and perished in the end, to be discredited by all history. Jesus trusted it and the wonder of his spirit lives on "the same yesterday, today and forever." Anybody could see Herod and Pilate and the soldiers of Caesar. They were altogether obvious, and their power to crucify the Master could not be denied. The staggering power of love, holding the world together and flowing like a mighty stream through the cosmos, was not so obvious. But Jesus trusted it, yielded his life to it, and now our knees bow before him and our tongues confess that he is Lord. Clearly, "the things that are seen are transient, but the things that are unseen are eternal." Why should any man lose heart worrying endlessly through the days?

CHAPTER IX

Antidotes for Discouragement

IN VIEW of the problems on the road to meaningful self-management it is not surprising that we blunder into times of discouragement. The pressures of life multiplied by our worries and tensions and frustrations often drive us down into the valley where the shadows of despair reach out to engulf us. We get what we call "the blues." A song popular some years ago strikes the mood:

> Blues, blues, twentieth century blues,
> Nothing to win or lose.

It is not a happy song, but lots of people sing it in one way or another. It usually ends with a whimper or perhaps a complaint. Nobody likes it much, but it is part of our twentieth-century emotional tone. It gets inside of us and gnaws at our bones. The very word "discourage" is discouraging. It means "to lessen courage, to deprive of confidence, to dishearten."

Blues are psychological. They are a state of mind. They may or may not flow from the experience of outward frustration. Either a headache or a hangover can induce mental depression. Physical or nervous exhaustion frequently paves the way for its unwanted coming. A love affair that has gone on the rocks is a choice inspirer of discouragement, and misbehaving children can drive us into the doldrums with the greatest of ease. Sickness, bad news, or a run of hard luck can send us along all draped in weeds, like a weeping willow tree. Certainly there is nothing like a stomach upset to turn the texture of the world to indigo, unless it be that morning-after-the-night-before sense of guilt that will not let us go.

None of us succeeds altogether in avoiding the blues. They descend upon us at unexpected moments, frequently for no apparent reason. The biographer of Audubon, the naturalist, comments that Audubon "always pursued a zigzag course between high elation and dark spirits." And it was Goethe who said that Beethoven was either "exulting to heaven" or "dejected to death." So are we all; but some are torn more than others by the contradiction of turbulent moods. "Sometimes I'm up, sometimes I'm down, Oh yes Lord" is an apt description of our feelings.

John Keats, obscurely born and troubled by a hereditary taint, frequently found himself in a state of discouragement. Under the spell of his depression he wrote:

> My spirit is too weak—mortality
> Weighs heavily on me like unwilling sleep,
> And each imagin'd pinnacle and steep
> Of godlike hardship, tells me I must die
> Like a sick eagle looking at the sky.[1]

Happily the fit of depression, which seized him suddenly, passed away shortly and he wrote to a friend, "Truth is, I have a horrid morbidity of temperament." He added, "It is, I have no doubt, the greatest enemy and stumbling block I have to fear."

We need not worry too much about our ups and downs as long as we are alternating between the two. It is more or less normal to zigzag between elation and dark spirits. There is trouble afoot, however, when our lives are all zig and no zag, all down and no up. When depression and discouragement are the prevailing winds by which we sail, it is time to look for a way out. Our moods are managing us and not the other way about. When we are living day after day in the shadow of our darkest moments, we are becoming neurotic. Perpetual pessimism is evidence of the fact that we are spiritually bilious, and in need of medicine more potent than luminal.

On the other hand, bland optimism is a little tiring. It lacks roots in realism. Whistling in the dark to keep up my spirit always leaves me disgusted with the fact that I cannot whistle on key. Pollyannas upset me. I am suspicious that maybe they are intent on making an impression! Life is too rugged to be sustained by superficial optimism that is comforted by the conclusion that things might be worse. They might be a lot better, too. Besides, I have seen too many bland optimists hit bottom with a thud and turn into perpetual pessimists. Sometimes I am a little frightened by people who go around spreading good cheer. They cannot seem to see that things will not turn out all right if we are just a little patient. They seem to think that problems will solve themselves, and come home quite happily, like Bo-Peep's sheep, "wagging their tails behind them." Just cheer up, and let's have a picnic! Every cloud has a silver lining!

To be sure, at times a bit of optimism is quite in place, when our pessimism is just a habit of mind. Some of our blues are more than a little perfunctory. We even get to the point where we enjoy our discouragement and take neurotic pleasure in dark moods. Queen Victoria once wrote discerningly: "How one loves to cling to one's grief." Her biographer notes that "She clung to it till it became her habit of morbid luxury, and out of it grew her . . . conviction that the state of her health would not permit her to do anything she found disagreeable."[2] Even superficial optimism would be a relief from that. If there is any choice between bland optimism and morbid pessimism, give me the optimism.

When we blunder into a zig of discouragement, it is helpful to recognize that the human body runs in cycles. There are times when we are at the crest of physical efficiency and other times when the graph line hits bottom. Our physical low tides are reflected in our minds and spirits. We cannot seem to do anything right and even our good intentions go wrong. The phenomenon makes headlines on the sports pages of newspapers. Babe Ruth's batting slumps were a national calamity, and when Joe Louis had an off night, countless words were dedicated to his poor timing, or his left-hand punches, which seemed to be short. When Bobby Jones played a poor round of golf, the world wondered if he had lost his magic touch.

Slumps are part of life. A pitcher who used to room with Joe DiMaggio recalls how one night he awoke to find a bed light on. DiMaggio's bed was empty, and the Yankee star, who was in the midst of a batting slump, was standing in front of a mirror, taking cuts at nonexistent pitches with an imaginary bat. Later DiMaggio observed, "Hitting's all timing. Your timing goes off and you're in a slump. You start pressing and you get into a rut. And then you come out of the slump without knowing it. You think you are doing the same things wrong and suddenly you're hitting."

It makes very little difference whether you are writing a book, singing, selling hardware, or playing baseball, there are times when you can't get a ball out of the infield. All you can manage is a little pop fly or a complete strike-out. It is discouraging and you would give almost anything to pull out of your slump. Then, without knowing why, you begin to tick again. You write with ease or you sing with power or you sell with relish and success. Quite possibly you have simply outrun a physical low and snapped back into good form. Until you come around there is not much you can do except keep on trying. To be sure, you need to remember to change your pace, sleep enough, play enough, and pray enough, but in all likelihood you still will have to wait out your slump.

It is helpful, too, to understand that your failures need not be final. Failure and defeat are discouraging, but you can rise above them both in the assurance that they are not the final words in your vocabulary. There is no failure except the failure to keep on trying. When you give up trying you blunder into despair, for in the moment of such surrender you do violence to the creative urge in yourself. The truth is strikingly illustrated in the life of F. Scott Fitzgerald, a creative novelist of the first order. He was both a product and a victim of the roaring twenties and the depressing thirties. After the triumph of *This Side of Paradise* there came the failure of *Tender Is the Night*. Critics were cool and indifferent. Financial failure and literary oblivion crushed Fitzgerald. Then his wife suffered a mental collapse and as a consequence of drink and worry Fitzgerald experienced a hardening of the creative arteries.

What troubled Fitzgerald most and was the source of his deepest despair was not his financial failure or his literary oblivion. "I had been," he wrote, "only a mediocre caretaker of most of the things left in my hands, even my talent." Under the stress of difficult circumstances he had betrayed his creative powers, surrendered to failure, and blundered into "the dark night of the soul." Before he died at forty-four he proved there was something tough and stubborn in him. He all but overcame drink and by 1940 was on the way back, his creative powers awakening from the death of his despair.

Most of the biographies of the world tell the stories of men and women whose failures were not final. Indeed, they were the ingredients of their greatness. Even in the midst of discouragement they refused to be mediocre caretakers of their talents. Like Abraham Lincoln, they took the leftovers of broken dreams and turned them into splendid achievements. Like Beethoven, they climbed to greatness on rungs of discouragement. They used their talents and kept on trying no matter how many failures they faced. They continued to grow in mind and in capacity through defeat and discouragement.

The truth is that "the dark night of the soul" can be preparation for renewal. Lewis Mumford put the idea aptly when he noted that a time of trouble is the time "to prepare for the renewal of life." It is a sobering fact of history that discouraging ages also have been eras of renewal. John Milton's greatest work was done amidst the chaos of England's Civil War. Walt Whitman's finest work came from the agony of our Civil War. Bunyan's *Pilgrim's Progress* came from Bedford Prison and the hurt of man's intolerance. Byron, Keats, and Shelley wrote while France and England were locked in war; and Goethe wrote himself into immortality while Napoleon's armies were pounding across Europe. So, in the midst of discouragement, prepare for "the renewal of life."

Abraham Lincoln caught the significance of preparation for renewal when he insisted that the reconstruction of our nation's Capitol go on even through the dark hours of war. When the Civil War began, the dome was still unbuilt. At the first inaugural, the Capitol grounds were cluttered with ladders and props and scaffolds, and the bronze statue of Freedom lay on the ground abandoned. The news of Bull Run, Antietam, and Chancellorsville did not stop work on the Capitol. There were those who insisted it was folly to go on building when the war was being lost. But Lincoln was adamant. By the time of the second inaugural the new Capitol was finished, and Freedom stood proudly in her place atop the structure. The finished work inspired Walt Whitman to write: "I like to stand aside and look a long, long time up at the dome; it comforts me."

It is this preparation for renewal even in the midst of discouragement and failure that gives us sanity and balance. Such preparation is an affirmation of our faith in the future, our confidence that failure is not final. Discouragement is not nearly so discouraging if it is relieved by preparation for a new beginning!

Closely allied to the preparation for renewal is the idea of useful creation. Purposeful creative activity is a remarkably effective antidote for the blues. "Only the artist," Beethoven once wrote, "or the emancipated scholar carries his own happiness about inside himself."[3] He meant to suggest that creative activity is an unceasing stimulus to joy. His comment is revealing and has bearing upon us who find so much of our entertainment vicariously. We do not sing or play the piano; we are entertained by radio or television. Conversation has become a lost art. Our "conversation pieces"—furniture, jewelry, or whatnot—are the last refuge of staggering minds. There was a lift in the conversation of "The Autocrat of the Breakfast Table," and the lilt of happy laughter in the talk that inspired the home of Bronson Alcott. The kindly schoolmaster was too busy with ideas to be blue about his disappointments in the conservative educational world of his time.

During the days of the depression when business was bad, my father made a corner of our basement into a workshop. He decided to make something. He did not know exactly what. He started by just whittling. In due time the block of wood he was whittling began to look like a bird. It was a poor specimen, but it had possibilities. Through the years of economic difficulty, my father repaired night after night to his workshop, where a collection of wooden birds, squirrels, and fish was taking shape. He made bluebirds and owls, blackbirds and wrens of wood and they were excellent imitations of the real thing. I have them now in my summer home where they add a touch of realistic beauty. Those birds were my father's creative answer to discouragement. If he could not create business, he could create artificial birds.

When we are restless and discouraged we turn to the movies to take our minds from our troubles for a while. Then we come home, quite as blue as we were before we went. Or maybe we hunt up a tavern to "kill time." We might better use time making something that will afford the satisfaction of creative achievement. A friend of mine learned to make silverware and turned out a whole dinner set of knives, forks, and spoons. He got over his blues in the process of creating something both useful and beautiful.

Recently I noticed an advertisement for a co-operative apartment. It was significant. It read: "Have all the comforts of home with none of the work." In such a home there is no place to putter, no need for "Mr. Fixit." And yet, the satisfaction of a home lies in what we do ourselves. The front porch we build is more than a front porch. It is a creative answer to the blues. The basement room we furnish ourselves is more than a rumpus room, it is a source of creative joy. Fixing the plumbing or putting in light plugs (with adequate respect for building codes) provides an outlet for the creative demands of the human spirit. Men must create or die spiritually.

As man's hours of work decrease, the need for creative use of leisure is imperative if he would avoid the blues. We have one of two choices: either kill time or use it creatively. Killing time is devastating; it leaves us with a sense of futility and waste. We go to seed when we ought to be flowering. Create something we must, if it is only a handy matchbox or a bed of flowers. Discouragement weighs heavily upon the man or woman who has nothing to do but kill time.

There is a curious paradox in the fact that discouragement comes upon us not only when we have too little to do but also when we are burdened by too much to do. Young mothers often are depressed by the endless round of washing bottles and diapers, feeding babies at night and tending them at all hours of the day and night. It seems too much, as if there were no end to toil. The years stretch endlessly ahead and no possibility of letting up appears on the horizon.

So it is with multitudes who toil ceaselessly to get ahead. There is no end to the work that needs to be done. If a man expects to get anywhere in the world's competitive struggle he must work more than a forty-hour week, with long week ends to relax. He must work hard, think hard and be willing to assume responsibility. But sometimes the load seems heavy to bear. Problems accumulate, correspondence piles up on the desk. What is worse, the office help doesn't seem to care.

There is a key, however, to digging out from a pile of work, and it is effective. Times without number it has saved me from discouragement and frustration, too. I keep telling myself, "One thing at a time, old boy." Maybe Theodore Roosevelt could manage half a dozen matters at the same time. I know I can't. Most of us can't. But we can take one step at a time. We can live one hour, one day at a time and make the most of it.

Years ago I climbed a rugged way to Abyss Lake, high in the Colorado mountains. I thought I never would reach my destination and several times I was on the verge of turning back. My feet were like lead and my pack weighed at least a short ton. Then I began to say: "One step after the other step. One step after the other step" in the rhythm of my climbing steps. It helped. After all, I could take only one step at a time, and I did not need to be discouraged about the endless steps ahead of me. One step at a time was enough. In due time I arrived at my destination, a glorious little lake where the trout were plentiful and ready to fight.

When you meet "just one of those days" when nothing goes right and work piles sky high, it is discouraging, I know. The desk is loaded, or the house is so torn up we wonder if we ever will manage to put things in shape. We have more than we can do. Nobody has any business expecting us to do so much! We get the nervous jitters just thinking of what we have to do. The simple fact is, however, that now, at this precise moment, we have but one task to do. There is one task that needs doing first, one job that demands performing now. Nothing else matters. Nothing else need concern us until it is done. What remains in the hopper for doing later has no bearing upon what must be done now. Five minutes from now, an hour from now, the next business will have its turn for our undivided attention. It, too, will join the growing ranks of tasks finished! One step at a time we move on until what must be done is done.

Discouragement comes, not from doing, but from brooding; not from work, but from thinking about work that needs to be done. Discouragement goes when mountains begin to melt, a shovelful at a time. Books are written a word at a time, one line after the other line; bricks are laid for the walls of a house one brick after the other brick; music is composed one note after the other note until a melody is born. No matter what we do we have to do one thing at a time, and only one. We cannot do more; we must not do less. One task done, added to another task done, adds up to creative accomplishment, to a sense of achievement. Discouragement turns, not into despair, but into exultation.

Obviously a sense of accomplishment is a vital antidote for discouragement. Maybe, like the boy Charles Dickens, you have to find a sense of achievement in being an expert at pasting labels on shoeblacking. Possibly the bride will have to find a sense of accomplishment in the cake that did not fail. Perhaps the teacher will have to find a sense of success in the one boy who responded eagerly to her intellectual prodding. It may be that the salesman must win a feeling of worth in the one sale he made in a barren day of failure.

It is fatal for us to accentuate our failures and minimize our accomplishments. I am sure I would have given up fishing for trout long since if I remembered only those discouraging days when I came home with an empty basket. I keep on fishing because I remember the wonderful days when I managed to outwit the well-educated fighters of the western streams and came home with "the limit." Despite days of failure, I put on my boots and head for the stream always hopeful that this will be "my day."

In one way or another we are constrained to live by the light of our best achievements and not in the shadow of our failures. Winston Churchill had a record of many failures before he reached his crowning triumph as Prime Minister of England in the critical years of his nation's history. But among the failures there were moments of solid success. He lived by the light of those moments of achievement in the faith that they represented what was possible. It was the same with Abraham Lincoln; though his failures were discouraging, he clung to his faith in himself by accentuating his accomplishments.

Notice a child learning to walk. He falls, often wailing in helpless indignation. With encouragement, he tries again. Then, in one glorious moment of triumph he takes three or four steps. The failures and the falls are forgotten then. Having succeeded once, he can do it again. He wants to walk, to go on walking. He may fall now and then, but the falls are incidental to the accomplishment. Each step he takes is a new affirmation of faith in his capacity to walk. So with life!

Many a college freshman, plagued by problems of adjustment, away from home for the first time, not knowing how to study, finds the first year discouraging. I remember one young man, a good student in high school, who went to college and failed to make a fraternity. Then he almost flunked his first semester. "I'm a failure," he said. "Well," I asked, "were you a failure in high school?" He confessed he did very well in high school. "You worked last summer, didn't you?" I asked. "Were you a failure on the job?" He assured me he was not a failure on the job. He had been asked to take the job again the next summer. He came close to a sense of utter failure because he was living under the shadow of his failure to make a fraternity. His achievements were obscured by a single defeat. When he began to see his situation in perspective he overcame his sense of discouragement.

One of the most gifted teachers I know blundered into a period of discouragement over a boy who caused her no end of embarrassment and trouble. She finally lost her temper in dealing with him, told him he was a disgrace to his family and to the school. As a consequence, the youngster greeted her daily with obvious hostility, and the problem was more complicated than before. She felt as if she had suddenly become a failure as a teacher. "Do you mean to say," I asked, "that one defeat in ten years of teaching makes you a failure?" "When you put it that way, it seems a little silly," she smiled. "But in this one case I have failed." "Perhaps so," I replied, "and yet, who does not fail now and then? The task of life is to learn something from our failures and not to be defeated by them."

Obviously we cannot afford to live in the shadow of our worst moments. I know from my own experience that preachers come upon Sunday mornings when everything goes wrong. The choir sings off key. The congregation is restless. The sermon goes out like a wet match. It is frightfully discouraging. Blue Mondays often follow on the heels of disheartening Sundays. However, if Tuesday, Wednesday, and Thursday are as blue as Monday, it is time for the preacher to accentuate his accomplishments for a while. There were Sundays when the sermon did not fail and the choir sang well and the congregation was responsive. There were Sundays when people were positively helped. The preacher is lost if he dwells in the darkness of his defeats.

It makes a vast difference whether you emphasize your failures or your accomplishments. Thomas Edison had the knack of seeing achievement even in failure. After several hundred experiments attempting to discover the secret of the incandescent lamp, he found encouragement in the knowledge that there were several hundred methods that would not work. To say the least, he had narrowed the experimental field. He had achieved knowledge of what would not work, and he could move in new directions. He was by no means dejected. So, in times of discouragement, we are wise to accentuate our accomplishments.

Again, in the face of discouragement, emphasize your personal assets. The trouble with failure is that it leads us to concentrate on our liabilities, on what we can't do. Actually, there are so many things I can't do that I have to keep my mind on the things I can do or I would be in a blue funk most of the time. When it comes to figures, I'm no good at all. When I add a column of figures I can get anywhere from one to three answers. I can't play the piano, tap dance, or even square dance. I can't fix the plumbing or make a garden grow. Thank heaven, there are a few other things I can do fairly well.

One of our major problems is to accentuate our assets while we are trying to overcome our liabilities. We all have limitations of mind and capacity, but it is a rare soul who is devoid of positive assets. Find out what you can do and do it with all your might! After ten years as a mediocre bond salesman, a friend of mine discovered he had a positive genius for running a ranch. He is happy as a lark working from dawn to dark raising cattle, mowing hay, and making a ranch pay for itself and then some. He is by no means miserable over the fact that he did not have the talent to be a successful bond salesman. He is grateful for his assets, for the talents that have made him a successful rancher.

Richard Mansfield, one of the great Shakespearian actors of all time, seemed to have rather meager talents as an actor. His primary assets were persistence and belief in his capacity to act. He wanted to act. Unhappily, he was poor and the chance of developing the talents he thought he had seemed remote. Nevertheless, he haunted the theater, doing chores backstage, pleading for a chance to act. At last his opportunity came. He was given a very small part in a London play. All he had to do was sit on a piano stool and speak two short lines. But when the curtain went up, he fainted and fell off the piano stool.

When he described his experience years later, he reported, "The reason I fainted was not because I was frightened, although I was very nervous. I fainted because I had eaten nothing for two days." He went on to say: "That night when I left the theater I was still hungry. The play director was furious, but a doorman gave me a sixpence and I bought a hot baked potato, the kind they sell on London streets. I carried it in my pocket to warm my hands. When it was cold, I ate it."

In concluding his story, Richard Mansfield remarked: "In spite of my failure and discouragement, I never lost faith in my dream." He never ceased to believe he could act, to believe in his talent. Even in failure he went on accentuating the assets he knew he had to offer the stage. Years later critics all over the world called him a genius, but he never would have risen above his discouragement if he had ceased to believe he had assets the theater could use.

In the presence of discouraging situations accentuate your achievements and your assets and, what is more, cultivate your appreciations. As the years go by and we come to the time of life when we meet what the Psalmist called "the destruction that wastes at noonday,"⁴ assets and achievements often lose at least some of their importance. You have climbed as high as you will in business, having passed "the point of no return." Henceforth promotions will go to younger men. There is little ahead for you except more of what you have already had. A friend of mine remarked concerning a teacher we both knew: "Jim has given up. He's just going through the motions of teaching until he retires a couple of years from now." That can happen to you more easily than you suspect. Your children are grown. They do not need you now. In fact, they hope in a kindly fashion that you won't be too much in the way. You will have enough to live on, a pension or some savings perhaps, and you won't need to worry. But there isn't any lift to your life and you feel discouraged.

It is not things you want. They are so lacking in permanence. It is strange the way we spend the first half of our lives struggling to get things and the second half wondering what to do with them. Nobody seems to want the treasures we could not wait to buy twenty or thirty years ago. They are not old enough to be antiques and yet they are too old for anyone to want very much. Having too much to take care of is a bother and sometimes we feel the truth of the saying: "Blessed be nothing." Not long ago at a wedding I wore an old pulpit robe without the velvet arm stripes, insignia of the doctor's degree. I thought with half a smile: How important those stripes seemed twenty years ago; how utterly unimportant now.

Life is like that, and it takes something more vital than things and more significant than honors to keep going beyond discouragement, beyond "the destruction that wastes at noonday." We need a deepened sense of values and cultivated appreciations to sustain our morale. Often we must swim against the tide, for our culture cultivates awareness of the things we have not at the expense of our appreciation of the best things in life —the things that are free. It infects us with "the huge army of the world's desires" and denies us the wonder of inexpensive enjoyment. Our wants multiply; our satisfactions diminish. Too many people have too many things to sell. Our descriptive adjectives become jaded from overuse. Colossal, magnificent, never-to-be-repeated bargains lure us hither and yon. Maybe God could get attention if He would dress up in neon lights on some busy corner or get Himself in the best and biggest magazines—in color, of course.

Our world has taken it for granted that "the finest, the biggest, and the best" make the biggest noise and the biggest splash. But in the economy of God it just isn't so. Nobody ever heard the sun go down in quiet glory, and the morning stars are too unobtrusive to be important when we are arranging a deal! Emerson understood the sublime meaning of little things that short-circuit discouragement. "When I bought my farm," he wrote, "I did not know what a bargain I had in bluebirds, bobolinks and thrushes which were not charged in the bill."[5] Such bargains are the secret of elation and inner joy.

Robert Easton tells the story of Thomas Ordway, a boy who lived on a farm, rejoicing in the warm sunlight, the fragrance of rain, and the beauty of his untroubled world. One day, haunted by the wonder of the world, he wandered through the chicken coops, through the corn fields, and on to the green grass. It put a tingle in his spine as he considered it all. Then, grabbing a fistful of dirt he rushed into the house where his mother was peeling carrots at the kitchen sink. Holding his handful of the good earth before him he said: "Gee, Ma, I love this stuff."[6] To be sure, the lad did not fully understand the wonder of God's glory in the creative genius of the good earth, touched by rain and sun, but there was in him

> That deep insight which detects
> The great things in the small.

and sees the glory of the commonplace.

"Beauty crowds us all our life" if we do not crowd it out. All about us, wherever we turn, there are sights and sounds to deliver us from maddening days of discouragement and frustration. Little children teach us that much. Edwin Vernon of Glasgow wrote some years ago in the *British Weekly* of a family with a custom I commend to you. It was started by the youngest member of the family, a little girl. One afternoon she was found busily writing something. Every little while she would cross out an item. Finally she finished her toil. She had prepared a list of "My Twelve Loveliest Things, People Not Counted."[7] Here is the list:

1. The cold of ice cream
2. The scrunch of dry leaves as you walk through them
3. The feel of clean clothes
4. Water running into the bath
5. Cool wind on a hot day
6. Climbing up and looking back
7. Hot water bottle in bed
8. Honey in your mouth
9. Smell of a drug store
10. Babies smiling
11. The feeling inside you when you sing
12. Baby kittens

That little girl found glory in the commonplace when she paused to "consider." There was a thrilling wonder in the ordinary.

A cousin in the family, a boy, and not many years older, constrained by example to consider, took up his pencil and wrote down his "Twelve Loveliest Things":

1. The feel of running
2. Looking into deep clear water
3. The taste of wild strawberries
4. A swallow flying
5. A clean hit in baseball
6. Water being cut at the bow of a boat
7. A mounted policeman's horse
8. An express train hurrying
9. A builder's crane lifting something heavy
10. The smell of wood
11. The feel of a dive
12. A thrush singing

Beat that if you can, you who were boys and girls twenty or thirty or forty years ago! What are your Twelve Loveliest Things?

"Consider the lilies of the field, how they grow."[8] These treasures of the field must have been among the lovely things Jesus cherished and enjoyed. They were avenues of enjoyment and satisfaction amidst the struggle and strain of his life. They cost him nothing. They made no noise to attract attention. They were simply there, small things, but testifying eloquently to something sublime behind them. The world is full of familiar things and experiences that are rich in enjoyment and meaning if we will "consider."

We need to check ourselves, now and then, to measure what we are missing. Without some mental and spiritual discipline our perceptions are dulled. Under the pressure of getting on and doing things, we often miss the values that relieve discouragement and make getting on worth the effort. We are in too much of a hurry to notice the "stars over a church tower" or "a perfect phrase."

Some months ago I went to an Illinois city to speak and my train was delayed an hour and a half by a derailed freight train. When I reached my destination, still in plenty of time for my engagement, I hurried four blocks west to my hotel, registered, and started up in the elevator with an elderly man wearing an ill-fitting uniform which proclaimed the fact that he was a bellboy. By way of conversation, he remarked: "Wasn't the sunset beautiful tonight?" I was almost ashamed to tell him I had not noticed. Then, apropos of nothing, he went on. "Time is a funny thing. When you are in a hurry you have too little of it, and when you are waiting for somebody you have too much of it." I had the uneasy feeling that he was gently rebuking me for being in such a hurry that I missed the sunset, which seemed very important to him.

Henry Thoreau found that his perceptions were being dulled by his labors and activities so he retreated to the quiet serenity of Walden Pond. He saw there what most of us never will see. One of the best pages from Thoreau's *Journal* is devoted to the eloquence of a cat's tail. Since reading Thoreau, I have been noticing cats' tails, and I have been amazed at their expressive eloquence. The sage of Walden Pond has another passage dedicated to the expertness of a squirrel stripping a pine cone, and the very last page of the *Journal* is a description of pebbles recently washed by rain. It is no wonder that Thoreau wrote that he found most of his heaven around him. He took time to notice.

Obviously, most of us cannot retreat to Walden Pond and spend our lives observing cats' tails and squirrels and pebbles. But there is a range of enjoyment and insight we do not need to miss. In times of discouragement, take time to see and feel and experience. Take time to "Consider the lilies of the field, how they grow." Stop long enough to notice the "flower in the crannied wall," to see the sunset, and to know the sea in all its moods—turbulence and rest, anger and joy, fury and stillness. Pause until you understand the love of a boy for his dog, until you can feel what he feels, and know that God is in that love.

Who can measure the enjoyment and the richness we miss because we do not see, because we hurry past the great things hidden in the small, the glory of God in the familiar. Lin Yutang describes travelers restlessly trying to get away from themselves, discouraged and discontented, going everywhere but seeing nothing, furiously rushing from Rangoon to Mandalay without learning anything or seeing anything. He notes they would be better off staying home, learning to see what is in their own back yards. There really is no use traveling without the capacity to see and to appreciate what you see. But then, he goes on, the capacity to see things "abolishes the distinction between travel to a distant country and going about the fields of an afternoon."

In truth,

> The poem hangs on the berry bush,
> When comes the poet's eye;
> The street begins to masquerade
> When Shakespeare passes by.[9]

But the poet and Shakespeare found time to "consider" and to await "the harvest of the quiet eye."

That brings us to the heart of the matter, namely, that God comes only to those who have the capacity to see Him in the ordinary and the familiar. There is a delightful touch in the make-believe story a small boy once told his father. "We were all going down the street," said the boy, "when suddenly, along comes God." There is more truth than humor in the lad's story. "Suddenly along comes God" in the song of a bird, the mystery of a snowflake, the handclasp of a friend, or the laughter of a child. "Along comes God," to lift us above our discouragement, but like as not we do not recognize Him when He comes.

As Robert Browning saw it, "Along comes God" into the drab lives of bewildered people through the song of Pippa, the silk winder's daughter, whose passing made things different. William Blake understood that "Along comes God" in the mating of the robin and the love-making of the dove. Thomas Carlyle felt that God came to him through Ralph Waldo Emerson, whose visit coincided with a low ebb in the fortunes of Carlyle. "He came like an angel," Carlyle wrote in his diary. "Along comes God" in the mystery of a peanut; George Washington Carver understood, and found God there. "Nay, whither can one look and not see him?" Thomas Kelly asked. "For field and stream and teeming streets are full of Him."[10]

> A haze on the far horizon,
> The infinite tender sky
> The ripe rich tint of the cornfields,
> And the wild geese sailing high.
> And all over upland and lowland
> The charm of the golden rod—
> Some of us call it Autumn
> And others call it God.[11]

"Suddenly along comes God" if our eyes have learned to see and our spirits to perceive. If we have learned to "consider the lilies of the field, how they grow," and to consider all the familiar commonplaces of our common days, we will find enjoyments to lift us and satisfactions to sustain us all our days. Deeper yet, we will find God. Nothing is ordinary, or drab, or uninteresting when God is in it! We never will be bored with life or deep in the misery of discouragement if we see God underneath life's surface and seeming.

If we have eyes to see and capacity to appreciate the hidden values around us we will find God where we are and in whatever we are doing. The Scriptures strike at the deeps in the word, "the place on which you are standing is holy ground."[12] If we are aware of that endless truth we possess a major ingredient of faith to manage our discouragement.

CHAPTER X

Get Off the Fence

THERE is a delightful episode in the life of Andrew Jackson, reported by Marquis James. A military review had been scheduled to take place on Boston Common, and Boston had been scoured for handsome mounts for the President and his suite. When the visitors appeared in front of the troops a salvo of artillery shook the earth. The borrowed horses reared and leaped. Jackson, a master horseman, controlled his mount superbly, and galloped along the line of troops. Cabinet officers and other notables followed as best they could. "Where is the vice-president?" Old Hickory asked, as he reined in his horse to take a salute. Riding alongside, his aide answered, "About as nearly on the fence as a man of his positive convictions can get."[1] Mr. Van Buren's bolting steed had brought up, tail first, against a fence and refused to budge.

Life often throws us into unmanageable situations and leaves us "on the fence." We find it incredibly difficult to make decisions, to choose between uninviting alternatives. The possibilities seem unattractive, even hazardous, no matter which way we jump. On one side of the fence is the frying pan and on the other the fire. We prefer not to decide, if we can avoid decision, so we remain in a state of suspended animation, often waiting until events take decision out of our hands. We do not often sense the fact that we decide, even though we decide not to decide. We decide by default, and the die is cast by our very indecision.

During the months before Abraham Lincoln became President, Buchanan, sitting in the White House, saw the clouds of Civil War approaching. Courageous leadership was needed, military and political decisions should have been made, but Buchanan sat "on the fence" and let things drift. However, as someone noted, "A policy of drift gathers only barnacles." While Buchanan waited, unable to decide what to do, the nation moved toward the chasm of violent conflict. In the end, Buchanan decided in favor of civil war, even though he decided not to decide.

Life is an unending series of decisions, choices between alternatives, and in life as in political affairs "a policy of drift gathers only barnacles." We decide between alternatives, or events decide for us. If we decide not to decide, we gather barnacles of indecision that hamper our capacity to decide anything. We blunder into the habit of indecision until we are perpetually on the fence, neither plus nor minus, but neutral on every occasion demanding action and choice.

To be sure, decision between alternatives often is difficult because most choices involve an element of "either-or." If we choose one thing, we cannot have something else. If we go here we cannot go there. If we do this we cannot do that. What is more, every choice we make is a crisis involving other choices. Dr. Harry Emerson Fosdick observes that once on a rutted country road he noted a sign which read: "Pick your rut carefully, you'll be in it for the next five miles." It is so in our experience. When we make a choice between alternatives we are likely to be in the rut we choose for some time to come. Choices have consequences, and, like Old Man River, they "just keep rollin' along."

When we are young it is not easy to choose a profession or a business, for if we choose to be a doctor we cannot be a plumber, or vice versa. If we decide to be a doctor, that choice involves a multitude of other choices, years of training and discipline, perhaps the postponement of marriage, possibly a life given in obedience to our calling so that we have no time of our own. When we choose to be married the choice is complicated by the fact that marriage is a long-range affair, "not just for a day, not for just a year, but always" as the old song has it. What is more, the decision to be married involves a whole series of decisions: the decision to pull in harness as part of a team, the decision to give up one kind of freedom for another, the decision to assume responsibility for someone else and possibly for children. If we decide, under strain, to be dishonest, that choice is not a simple one. We are likely to be in the dishonest rut for a long time to come and our dishonesty will involve a series of other dishonesties and deceptions in order to keep it under cover or to justify it if it comes to light.

Because our choices are so exclusive, giving us "either-or" alternatives, because they determine the way of our going for a long time to come, and because they involve other choices, we resort to various expedients to avoid the necessity for choice. Sometimes we try to postpone decision. Maybe if we wait long enough we can escape the necessity for choosing. A German minister took that road in the days when Hitler was riding to triumph in the Fatherland. To oppose the Nazis was dangerous, but his conscience would not let him go along. So he tried to be neutral. But he found himself swept into the Nazi tide, going along, having decided in favor of the Nazis even though he had decided to postpone choice.

Or, possibly because any choice we make involves hazards we do not like, we try to carry water on both shoulders. We will put one foot in heaven and keep the other securely anchored to the earth. We will please everybody by being "all things to all men." We will not be caught declaring ourselves one way or the other. Stephen Douglas tried to sit on the fence, to straddle the slavery issue in his famous debates with Abraham Lincoln. After Douglas had been elected to the United States Senate, Lincoln noted that Douglas had managed to be supported as the best instrument both to break down and to uphold the slave power. But, said Mr. Lincoln, "No ingenuity can keep this deception up a great while."[2] He was right, and the career of Mr. Douglas floundered in the shallow waters of his own indecision. Like John Bunyan's "Mr. Facing Two Ways," he blundered into failure. So do we all.

Sometimes we try to silence those who disturb us with invitations to declare ourselves. Socrates was forced to drink the fatal hemlock because he disturbed the corrupt society of Athens with annoying invitations to practice justice. The martyrs of history were martyrs because they challenged comfortable people to get off the moral fence and declare themselves. Bernard Shaw caught our mood in his *Joan of Arc* when he pictured Charles nearly distracted over Joan's upsetting influence. She was forever demanding righteousness and truth. Irritated beyond measure he says: "Why doesn't she shut up or go home?" No doubt the religious leaders of Jerusalem felt that way about Jesus. They did not want to meet issues. They had no desire to face their own self-deceptions. Why didn't Jesus keep still or go home? Instead, however, he always "appeared to be going further."[3] We know from our own experience that Jesus will not go home and he will not keep still. He refuses to abdicate. That fact keeps us awake nights struggling with moral alternatives. Life would be simpler if there had been no Sermon on the Mount and no ideals to bother us. If we could wipe out all memory of the Master we could decide to please ourselves and let it go at that. If he would please keep still or go home we would not need to struggle with moot questions.

In our time, we have devised another way of avoiding moral decision. We have put the accent on tolerance and broad-mindedness. We have even tried to escape the high demands of Jesus by turning him into an innocuous good fellow, à la Bruce Barton. "The Man Nobody Knows," under the light touch of Mr. Barton, became a modern man about town, a thoroughly broad-minded fellow. He loved everybody, forgave everybody, cheered up everybody with easy good grace. He never really was hard on anyone except the Pharisees. He even forgave the woman in adultery, didn't he? He told a story of a Prodigal Son who was forgiven and welcomed home. He forgave Zacchaeus, a dishonest taxgatherer. Really, Jesus was a genial good fellow and he need not bother us much. What we forget is that the price of forgiveness was a cross and its evidence was moral recovery.

Nevertheless, the picture of Jesus as a broad-minded good fellow fits our mood. We have lifted tolerance to the position of virtue-in-chief. We can forgive anything but intolerance. Beat your wife if you must and steal if you please, but by all means be broad-minded. Don't go overboard for righteousness, or truth, or anything else for that matter. There was an account in the papers about a man who divorced his wife to marry an Egyptian dancer. When somebody asked the wife what she thought of her husband's behavior she remarked: "Oh, it is perfectly all right. I just hope he will be happy." She seemed to be saying: "Oh, anything goes in this world and we had best be tolerant about it."

By enshrining the virtue of tolerance we avoid the necessity for moral decision. We believe, for example, that people would be better off if they did not drink. But we want to be broad-minded. So we go to cocktail parties to celebrate whatever needs celebrating, from the sacrament of marriage or baptism to our latest promotion. Then we wonder why so many people are having to scramble into Alcoholics Anonymous in search of salvation. In the name of tolerance we teach Junior to drink like a gentleman and then wonder why Junior becomes a problem. We condone corruption on the assumption that after all in politics a favor deserves a favor, even a mink coat. Then we wonder why we have to pay such frightful taxes. We accept gambling as a respectable vice and then wonder why good citizens are brutally beaten for trying to keep their communities free of gangsters. Be anything you please, but for goodness' sake, don't be intolerant! Broad-mindedness in our time has become a means of sitting on the fence virtuously. No longer do we really need to struggle over moral issues. We simply retreat into the elysium of broad-mindedness, where we need not bother about moral imperatives, or stern principles, or standards for judgment.

Nevertheless, broad-mindedness leaves us living in the shallows where there is no depth, and life has nothing to undergird it. Someone described the power of Gladstone by saying that "he lived from a great depth of being." He was not tolerant. He had deep convictions that motivated his life. His convictions gave him strength and courage for great leadership. Maybe some day we will learn that there is no strength of character, no power for great living, without great conviction. Can you imagine Mr. Milquetoast being a man of power? He has no convictions. He will not risk a clear-cut decision on anything. He is tolerant with a capital "T." The tragedy of Mr. Milquetoast is that he is perpetually on the fence. Like Cowper's friend,

> He would not with a preemptory tone
> Assert the nose upon his face his own;
> With hesitation admirably slow,
> He humbly hopes, presumes, it may be so.[4]

Great lives always rest on great decisions that motivate and drive. Jesus faced life as it might have been in the shallows.

He considered the greatest temptation life brings to anyone, the temptation to be broad-minded concerning evil. He met it in the wilderness where he toiled with his own soul all night—yes, for forty nights. He met the temptation with vital decision: "You shall worship the Lord your God, and him only shall you serve."[5] He arrived at decision in depth and decision was the source of his power. He knew that broad-mindedness and sentimental tolerance would turn him into a weakling, not a man of strength, certainly no savior.

Dr. Robert Goodrich notes that anyone who has neither convictions nor opinions inevitably gives the impression of weakness. He observes that even in simple things like ordering breakfast that is true. You have a guest and you say to him, "How would you like your eggs this morning?" "Well, just any way. It doesn't matter." "Yes," you say, "but would you like them fried or scrambled?" You feel slightly annoyed when the answer comes, "Well, just any way. It doesn't make any difference." "All right," you say, "I'll fry them. But do you like them sunny side up or turned over?" "Oh, just any way." So you fry the eggs wishing you were not too polite to throw them. What impression do you get of your guest—an impression of strength or of weakness? Clearly, life has no power, no strength, without capacity to decide. As the Scriptures have it. "He that wavereth is like a wave of the sea."[6]

Of course there is always the danger of wrong decision. One of the hazards of freedom in anything is the possibility of wrong choice. Sometimes, to be sure, there are moral choices to which there are no alternatives. The right and the wrong, the wise and the unwise stand out with crystal clarity and we say: "I can do no other." But there also are times when decisions and choices depend on knowledge and information that must be diligently sought. Quite possibly Jesus had complex situations in mind when he said: "You shall love the Lord your God with . . . all your mind."[7] Certainly wise conclusions and judgments involve the persistent use of the mind, as a retired schoolteacher acknowledged when she remarked she would like to write a book on the theme: "Is Your Mind an Asset?" The question is an important one and we ought to address it to ourselves while we are trying to get off the fence with wise decision.

Time and again my father used to say to me: "Son, use your head." "Think." The advice was sound, but it presupposed a fund of knowledge and information basic to thinking and using my head. As he saw the matter, loving God involved putting into my mind the resources of information and inspiration that are the foundation for sound judgment. Herbert Spencer noted wisely that "Mental power cannot be gotten from ill-fed brains." Sometimes we say, perhaps facetiously, that "Ignorance is bliss." It is nothing of the sort. It is an invitation to misery. John Wesley is said to have received a letter once from a pious brother who declared: "The Lord has directed me to write you that while you know Greek and Hebrew, he can do without your book larnin'." Mr. Wesley replied appropriately, "Your letter received, and may I say in reply that your letter was superfluous, as I already knew that the Lord could do without my learning. I wish to say that, while the Lord does not direct me to tell you, yet I wish to say to you on my own responsibility, that the Lord does not need your ignorance either."

Ignorance is a liability, but a well-fed mind is a priceless resource for sound judgment and wise decision. Therefore, when you are on the fence, you had best begin by digging out whatever information there is that bears on your problem. Sometimes we say: "Let your conscience be your guide," but it is important to add: "Let the evidence guide your conscience." It is folly to remain forever on the fence, but it is also folly to leap to wrong conclusions unsupported by available facts. The prejudices, biased opinions, and uncritical convictions that litter the social landscape are simply conclusions that have crystallized without evidence to sustain them. They are sources of grave danger in our time.

We smile at children sometimes because their conclusions so often are not supported by the facts. When I was a small boy, walking along the sidewalk, one of my playmates cautioned me about stepping on the cracks between blocks of cement. Said he, "Step on a crack and you'll break your mother's back." Thereafter, for weeks I cautiously avoided stepping on cracks until I noticed that my father seemed utterly unperturbed by sidewalk cracks and his mother's back was quite sound. The plain evidence at hand simply did not support my naïve and childish conclusion, so I abandoned the conclusion.

Wise decision and choice demand a willingness to modify our conclusions in obedience to the evidence. Unfortunately, the older we grow the more difficult that becomes unless we have cultivated the habit of respecting evidence. Shortly after its publication I had a letter roundly denouncing the new Revised Standard Version of the Bible as a device of the devil. After all, the writer noted, "The King James Version of the Bible is God's word and nobody has any right to tamper with it." The conclusion, however, is altogether unwarranted by the facts. Most of us love the King James Version of the Bible. We grew up on it. But the King James Version is a seventeenth-century translation of ancient manuscripts written in Hebrew, Greek, or Aramaic. The new Standard Version is simply a better translation of the earliest manuscripts available. The decision to use or to condemn the new translation obviously should rest on facts and not on fancies.

Freedom depends on the clear thinking of citizens everywhere, and democracy is imperiled by minds that habitually arrive at conclusions unrelated to the facts. But unfortunately it is infinitely easier to arrive at decisions and conclusions when we have a minimum of evidence than when we have a maximum of evidence. We can sympathize with the justice of the peace described by Rexford Mitchell. The good justice was judging a lawsuit and the attorney for the plaintiff had nearly concluded his argument. "Counsel," the justice interrupted, "it will not be necessary for you to proceed further. You have convinced me. I have made up my mind." Of course the attorney for the defense protested vigorously. "Certainly you are going to hear the defendant's side of the story." "No," the justice answered, "I've made up my mind. If I listened to you it might confuse me. So, I guess I won't."[8]

Actually there are those who find an illusory security in one-sidedness. They have discovered that if they shut out one half of the truth they can feel secure in clinging to the other half. But such security is a fool's paradise. Christopher Fry spoke the truth in his play *The Firstborn* when he made Moses say to a stubborn Pharaoh,

> A man must be more than a Pharaoh.
> He must dare to outgrow the security
> Of partial blindness.[9]

Precisely so. Partial blindness makes difficult problems very simple. Thirty years ago, for example, I knew all the answers to the social issues of the era. World problems were quite simple. Just get people to be pacifists and that would end war. Just give labor a decent wage and that would bring the millennium in industrial relations. It was all so plain. Now I am not so sure. The more I accumulate evidence and outgrow my "partial blindness," the more I discover that the problem of human relations is not so simple as it seemed thirty years ago when my conclusions were arrived at with a minimum of information.

Nevertheless, dependable conclusions demand willingness to

examine all the evidence we can discover by diligent search. If you have decided you are an atheist, you ought to examine the beliefs of the Christians and study the evidence in nature and history and in lives made rich. If you decided to be a Christian, you ought to face the problems of faith until you can "give to any man a reason for the faith that is in you." If you have concluded that the "One World" philosophy is essential, you ought to read the Chicago *Tribune* to get the opposite point of view. If you tend to be an isolationist, you ought to read the New York *Times* to get the other side of the question. If you are an employer, you ought to listen to the labor commentators on the radio, and if you are a union member, you ought to listen to the arguments of commentators who see things from industry's point of view.

Another basic requirement for wise decision and choice is independence and, if need be, courage to think in opposition to the crowd. Independent intellectual integrity is the mark of a free mind. What is more, it is the necessary foundation for freedom. But it is not easy to achieve and it takes courage to maintain. Mrs. Percy Shelley felt the problem when the time came to choose a school for her son. She was advised to send him to a school where he would learn to think for himself. "To think for himself," she cried. "Oh my God, no, teach him to think like other people." After living with Percy Shelley, the intellectual rebel, she had had enough of independent thinking.

It is infinitely easier to think like everybody else than it is to think with independent intellectual integrity. Independence usually means opposition. When Jesus came preaching, it was apparent that he was thinking independently. "You have heard that it was said. . . . But I say to you . . ."[10] was his formula, and it ran head on into the entrenched thinking of his day. Jesus was off the beaten track, blazing new trails, pointing to new horizons, and the crowd and its leaders shouted, "No." The men in the crowd surrounding Pilate's palace were thinking alike. Their minds were like peas in a pod when they shouted, "Crucify him. Crucify him."

But over and over again in history the independent minds have pointed the way to progress. It was Galileo, thinking in opposition to the entrenched beliefs of his time, who brought to mankind new insight into the nature of the universe. It was Columbus, thinking independently, who dared to challenge the almost universal belief that the world was flat. It was Voltaire, thinking independently, who challenged the claim of kings to rule by divine right. It was Thomas Jefferson, thinking independently, who laid the foundations for our freedom. We can thank God for men of independent intellectual integrity who dared not to think as others did.

Quite possibly the crowd will not cheer your best decisions and choices between alternatives. You may have to stand alone. Charles Francis Berry, an American League umpire for some years, observes that making decisions on a baseball diamond is a hazardous business. He says he is puzzled sometimes by the spectators. "It seems," he remarks, "that you get your biggest yelp from the crowd on some of your best decisions." That is life in a nutshell. The prophets knew that, and Jesus knew it. You get your "biggest yelp from the crowd on some of your best decisions." The crowd howled "No" when Lincoln faced the end of the Civil War "with malice toward none and charity for all." The crowd howled "No" when Paul joined the Christians and when Woodrow Wilson pleaded for peace without vengeance.

It is altogether apparent that sound decision requires a relentless pursuit of information plus a quality of independent integrity. It also is obvious that the mind requires a dependable standard for judgment. Even when our information is complete and we are quite willing to be out of step with the crowd, we seldom have clear-cut choices between what is all good and all bad, between black and white. We have to choose between shades of gray. We are like a baseball umpire, calling balls and strikes on batters. It is not often that the ball cuts the middle of the plate, midway between the shoulders and the knees of the batter. Most pitched balls cut the corners of the plate. They are almost too low or too high. So the umpire makes mistakes, and now and then batters or pitchers protest, sometimes with heat and fury. The question is one of judgment, and many times a pitched ball might be called either a ball or a strike.

Nevertheless, the umpire never remains on the fence. He calls balls and strikes with the voice of authority and certainty. He may have some shade of inner doubt, but his decision is firm and he sticks to it regardless of the protests. To be sure, the protests may very well inspire more careful judgment; they should do so. However, neither protests nor faulty judgment alter the basic standard by which the umpire determines balls and strikes. A pitched ball is a strike if it comes over the plate between the knees and the shoulders of the batter. Nobody questions the standard of judgment. Umpires, batters, and pitchers give unswerving allegiance to the standard, for without it baseball could not be played.

Like baseball, life decisions and choices demand a standard for our judgment of values. Inevitably, the nature of our decisions will be determined by the yardstick we apply. If our standard of judgment is self-interest, our choices between alternatives will be altogether determined by what we think is good for us. Of course, that standard is a precarious one because our interests seldom coincide with the interests of others, and the only solution to a conflict of interests is the capacity to win the conflict by hook or by crook. To establish self-interest as the standard of judgment by which we make choices would be like a batter's insisting that a strike must be pitched to the precise spot he wants it. But baseball could not be played on any such terms.

Or suppose our standard of judgment is party interest. The Communists give a striking illustration of what happens when that standard is applied. The rights to "life, liberty and the pursuit of happiness" are altogether limited to those who compose the proletariat. There is no right to protest against purges or exile, the appropriation of private property, or any action of the party designed to promote its own interest. Democracy sometimes is undermined by the theory that party interest is primary and therefore choices are to be made in terms of the welfare or the power accruing to the party. But that is like saying that for one team on the baseball diamond the pitcher must put the ball through the middle of the plate, while the other team gets the benefit of the corners of the plate. Neither baseball nor life can be played that way.

In life it is clear that we make choices and decisions on the basis of many different standards. The prophets of Israel would say that we are worshiping false gods, for in reality our standard of judgment becomes the god we worship. It may be self-interest, wherein we worship ourselves. It may be party interest, wherein we worship the party as lord of life. It may be the family, the class, the race. It may be business or profession. It may be the gratification of any single desire that sweeps into our ken and becomes the center of our concern. Whatever becomes the standard by which we choose between alternatives becomes the god we worship.

We worship false gods, however, unless the standard we adopt is a safe and wise standard not only for ourselves but also for everyone else as well. When you face the necessity for decision between alternatives, would you be willing for all others to use the same standard in making their choices? What would happen to society if your standard of judgment became universal? When you choose vengeance rather than forgiveness on occasions of hurt feelings, what would happen to society if everyone adopted feelings as the standard for judgment? When you choose dishonesty rather than integrity in order to secure a profit, what would happen to society if everyone adopted private profit as the sole standard by which choices are made? When you neglect your family for the sake of your social life, how would society fare if everyone made social prestige the standard for making choices?

Clearly, wise choice is quite impossible apart from a standard of judgment that is capable of being applied to all men everywhere. That is why, as Abraham Lincoln said, freedom is possible only where it is "freedom under God." Our freedom to choose between alternatives is altogether dangerous unless it is guided by a standard rooted in our loyalty to God. The Ten Commandments, as a standard of judgment, are valid because "under God" they have a universal reach. We can break them, but they will break us if we do. They are objective standards, rooted in the nature of God's world. The Beatitudes as a standard of judgment are not sentimental; they are ultimately sound. We can call balls and strikes in life on the basis of them, knowing they are rooted in the mind of God and worthy to be universal—anywhere, any time.

When you are "on the fence," trying to choose between alternatives, you are lost without a standard of judgment more basic than your own desires, or feelings, or interests. If you have no worthy standard yourself, you cannot trust others, for you will suspect that their choices are fashioned on foundations no more ultimate than your own. You will suspect their motives because you cannot trust your own. You will doubt the decency of others because you doubt your own. As Voltaire noted, "If there is no God, all is permitted"—permitted, indeed, because nothing is ultimate. Truth is simply an instrument to serve your purpose, and if it does not serve your purpose, a lie will do as well. Good will is merely a means by which to "win friends and influence people," and on occasions when hard-boiled coercion will serve your purposes more adequately you can be quite ruthless. Nothing is really better than anything else. Being yourself the ultimate arbiter of balls and strikes you can call them as you please regardless of standards.

Fundamentally, we are constrained to decide whether we think the Master's way will lead us to God and to wisdom and sound judgment. It will be mostly a matter of faith. We cannot prove it until we travel his way to see for ourselves. We have to do our own traveling and our own believing. We seldom can know the ending of an adventure from the beginning. The best we can do is to learn what we can from one who has traveled the way and left at best a rough map for our guidance.

Long years ago I went on a hike with two others to a tiny lake high in the Colorado mountains. We had heard of the wonderful trout playing deep in its icy waters. Carrying sleeping bags and fishing equipment on our backs we toiled up a steep trail until we came to a place where the trail divided. One branch moved off into a lovely valley and the other turned sharply up the side of a mountain. We paused there for a moment, wondering. At that fork in the trail we had a decision to make. Indeed, we had two very important decisions to make. We had to decide where we were going. Were we going on to the lake we had set out to find? Or were we going somewhere else? We had to decide, then, which trail would take us where we wanted to go. Should we push on straight ahead or turn sharply to the right. Which trail would take us to the lake? We had to decide.

Sooner or later we come to that fork in the road and we have two decisions to make. First, we cannot go anywhere in life until we decide where we are going, what ends we seek. Do we want God? Do we want God's love and forgiveness and peace, or do we want a bit of tinsel that will tarnish almost before we have won it? Do we want life lived from the depths of being in God, or life in the shallows where we will find nothing but snags and weeds and swamp? Do we want love and loyalty, truth and integrity, or do we want a handful of fool's gold that is worth nothing when we have it assayed?

"Choose this day whom you will serve"[11]—yourself and your own little aims, or God and the dreams He made vivid in Christ. Make it concrete, if you will. You have to decide whether you want life with God that dares to be open and unafraid or life in the shadows. In the field of diplomacy, Woodrow Wilson talked much of "open covenants" between nations "openly arrived at." He insisted quite rightly that there was no reason for secret diplomacy unless you had something to hide. Paul put the idea quite simply and yet profoundly when he said "as children of light" walk ye "in the light."

Do you have to hide what you are thinking of doing? We have seen enough in our time of hidden things, under-the-table deals, secret influence-peddling at a price, bribery, corruption, and all the rest. We know what it costs. You can have that if you want it. You can have the glitter of secret things, until the glitter wears off and you hate yourself. You can have the hell of the secret, for hell is mostly the inability to live with your secrets, or you can have the heaven of life lived in the light with God. Make up your mind what you want. You can have it. Make up your mind where you are going! You can get there.

To be sure, when you have decided where you are going you have to decide which trail will take you there. You have to decide which trail will take you to the shallows and which one to the deeps. When we came to the fork of the mountain trail we had only the word of a man who had been where he wanted to go. He told us that when he came to the forks we would have to go up the trail to the right. We took it on faith, faith in his word. We launched out, not knowing for sure, but believing.

It is so with life. You cannot be sure that integrity always pays. Sometimes it does not seem to pay. You have to take it on trust. You cannot be sure that "Love never fails."[12] Often it seems to fail. You cannot prove that "virtue is its own reward." Sometimes it seems to have no reward but loneliness. You cannot prove that they who "hunger and thirst for righteousness"[13] shall be filled. You cannot be dead certain that going the second mile, beyond the demands of duty, is worth what it costs. You have to take it on faith, faith in the word of one who traveled the trail from the beginning to the end and made life glorious on the way.

One thing is certain: When you come to some fork in the road and the Master calls: "I am the way,"[14] you can know he has been over the road. He did not preach the Sermon on the Mount from an ivory tower, set apart from the world. He preached from the rich variety of his own living experience. Because he spoke from the depths of his own knowledge he could risk saying: "If any man's will is to do his will . . . he shall know."[15] And so it is. But you have to decide.

So we come to the final issue, to the goal of our striving and seeking. Life seems to say that we were born to overcome our frustrations and fears, our tensions and anxieties, our insecurity and our indecision. We were born to grow, to mature in mind and spirit, and to be something worthy inside. But what is the end of our living, the reason for courage and faith and the character that holds the world together?

CHAPTER XI

Your Reason for Living

STANDING in a cemetery some time ago I noted scores of tombstones, each bearing a name and two dates. One weather-beaten stone bore the name of a man and the dates 1860-1941, a period of eighty-one years. Vast changes took place in the world during those years. The horse and buggy surrendered to the automobile and the pony express succumbed to the telephone and the telegraph. Victorian moral standards were challenged by the march of relativity and ideology became a popular substitute for theology.

As I meditated there in the cemetery, I wondered about the man whose name marked the tombstone before me. How did he manage the strains of his changing world? Was he one of the many like those Matthew described as "harassed and helpless" in a troubled world? Was life for him a wearying struggle to get from one day to the next, or did he grow in knowledge and insight, character and courage as he marched from 1860 to 1941? Was his life a burden or a joy? He must have known the ills to which all flesh is heir, and the tensions that come with adjustment to a changing world. Did he die defeated and bitter, or triumphant?

I could not know the answers to my questions because I

could not ask the dust for answers. Yet, I dare say that what life meant once to the man whose tomb I surveyed hinged on whether or not he felt some vital and compelling reason for living. Did he find significant meaning in his toil and suffering? Somewhere along the road of his life he had to answer for himself the questions that confront all of us. Is life simply a matter of blundering from one day to the next, or is it a great adventure with meaning and purpose at its heart? Is it merely a dull, uninspiring affair of struggle and toil that means nothing, or is it a stirring quest for what Carl Sandburg calls "keepsakes, lasting beyond hunger and death"?[1]

We can't find the answers just doing a sum. There's no proof one way or the other, really. We "live by faith and not by sight" or we do not live at all. There is no way to summon all the evidence that life has meaning and put Q.E.D. at the end. The evidence is in life itself, in the difference between life that is inspired by faith in its meaning and life that is undermined by a sense of utter futility. Life is, as Shakespeare said, "a tale told by an idiot" if, for us, it signifies nothing.

We are beginning to understand that "Man cannot live by bread alone."[2] There is a growing conviction that it takes more than bread to lift us above our frustrations and tensions, our fears and discouragements. We are searching for meaning, reaching out "beyond the prison of the five senses" for something to give life a lift. We simply are not satisfied with life devoid of purpose, and we are weary of being lost in small matters, as J. P. Marquand noted in his play *Point of No Return*. One of the principal characters observed of another, "He knew all the little answers, but he missed the large questions." He knew how to get ahead in business and how to keep life well dressed and upholstered. So do we, but we know the little answers are not enough. The big questions concern us: What is it all about? How does a man find high meaning for his life?

Plays like *Point of No Return* are by no means isolated, crying alone in the wilderness that life must have meaning. On the contrary, one evidence of the new mood of our time is an apparent trend in literature and drama that may be described as a search for meaning. Harry Hansen, the literary critic, noted it recently when he wrote that we are now in a decade "in which the true writing note will be a searching of heart for sound values, a stress on courage rather than on ruthlessness, and a reaffirmation of the ability of man to make wise decisions." It is implicit in *The Caine Mutiny* and in *The Old Man and the Sea,* and it crops out in Faulkner and Steinbeck, "despite the heavy load of naturalism they carry and their determination not to be conventional."[3]

It should be added, too, that the large increase in books on religious subjects is further indication of a quest for food more sustaining than bread. In our decade more people are reading religious books than ever before. They are searching for spiritual meaning in a bewildering world. They feel the need Sherlock Holmes expressed when he said to his friend and colleague, "My dear Watson, you are my one fixed point in a world of change." So it is that our decade is clamoring for dependable points of value in which to find meaning and purpose in struggle.

There is a second suggestive trend which is indicative of our awareness that meaning is essential in industry's discovery that it takes more than wages and reasonable hours to satisfy the spirit of the modern worker. Industry is learning that men and women are something more than marketable mannequins. They are also persons in search of meaning and significance for their lives. While they bear what Paul called "the image of the earthly" and therefore seek the means by which life can be sustained, they also bear "the image of the heavenly," and therefore seek spiritual meaning to provide their toil with significance. We are both dust and divinity!

After twenty-five years of experiment that began more by accident than by design, the Western Electric Company discovered the power of a sense of meaning in a job and the importance of seeing divinity as well as dust in workers. Western Electric set out to demonstrate the effect of lighting on production. The results, however, were not what the experimenters expected. When light was increased, production in the test room increased. That was in accordance with expectations. But when the light in the test room was reduced even below the normal standard, production increased again.

The surprised experimenters began seeking other factors that might bear on production. Possibly better working conditions were the answer. In another experiment, instead of decreasing the light they decreased working hours. Production in the test room went up. Morning and afternoon rest periods were introduced. Production climbed higher. Rest periods were lengthened and free lunches served. As expected, production continued to climb. Then the plan was reversed. Workers in the test room toiled forty-eight hours a week with no rest periods, no lunches, no favors. Production remained as high as ever.

The whole experiment seemed futile. But was it? Possibly there was some hidden factor that could explain what seemed utterly irrational. Perhaps there was an intangible secret that involved the very nature of human personality. Professor E. J. Roethlisberger of the Harvard Business School pointed to the fact that each worker in the test room found new personal significance in the fact that he was being used in an important experiment. Even standing beside an impersonal machine had meaning in relation to the search for knowledge. Workers found satisfaction and even inspiration in the discovery that their toil had meaning for themselves and others. They responded by giving their best to their toil.

It is significant, too, that in the five years preceding 1954 about forty major commercial enterprises hired chaplains to minister to the spiritual needs of their personnel. What is more, prayer meetings or other devotional services of interfaith character are held regularly in at least one thousand companies throughout the country. Laymen's groups, formed by businessmen for the purpose of applying spiritual values to industrial and community problems, have sprung up in more than a score of cities.

There seems to be one central idea behind the new emphasis on spiritual life: the belief that worship and prayer help to put a sense of meaning and purpose in life and thereby contribute to the peace of mind and the inner satisfaction men and women find in their toil. Rollin M. Severance, president of the Severance Tool Industries of Saginaw, Michigan, testifies to the value of a fifteen-minute devotional service in his plant each morning. He says, "These services have brought a spirit of brotherhood into the plant, because there are no classes under God's laws and prayer brings all men together. People like to work here because of the kinship and peaceful conditions created by prayer."[4]

Kinship in a common task under God provides an essential conviction of meaning in toil that lifts work above mere plodding from day to day and gives it an eternal reach. In an atmosphere of spiritual concern that goes beyond material value "deep calleth unto deep," and men respond with enthusiasm and inner satisfaction.

The third piece of evidence that we are becoming aware of our need for a sense of meaning in our lives is in our own personal seeking for something to make life worth living. There is a suggestion of our feeling in the play *Morning's at Seven,* in which Carl, a white-haired dentist, periodically suffered from what the family politely called "spells." When the "spells" came on he went about frantically asking everyone, "Where am

I?" The question did not concern his geographical location. He knew precisely where he was with reference to his home or the corner drugstore. What troubled him was a far deeper matter: "Where am I after sixty years of living? What have I accomplished? What have I done with my possibilities? Where am I spiritually, mentally and morally speaking?" He was haunted by the feeling that he had been going nowhere through the years even though he owned his home and had a comfortable living.

Often we are disturbed by the questions that bothered Carl. We have food and shelter and clothes to wear. We live in homes that are reasonably comfortable, but still we feel cheated. We do not go around asking everybody we meet, "Where am I?" but the question is there in our minds. We wonder. We look back over the years, along the road we traveled. We went to school, got a job, got married, raised a family, but where are we now? We may have saved enough to provide for our needs to the end of our days. Maybe a pension or an annuity will see us through the sunset years. But there is something missing. As a thoughtful man put it once, "I feel as if I had lived through everything but life." We have everything and yet nothing that satisfies our deepest yearning. T. S. Eliot sensed the feeling when he wrote,

> We are the hollow men,
> . . . .
> Headpiece filled with straw.[5]

I recall being deeply troubled one evening at one of the swank clubs of Chicago, where I watched a crowd of successful businessmen celebrating something or another. Most of them were in their cups. I kept asking myself why? Was success so devoid of meaning it had to be escaped? Were the tensions and pressures of business life so great they could not be endured?

Why were these successful businessmen, some of them outstanding, making fools of themselves? They would have been incredulous if they had been told they were running away from a meaningless existence. Really they were having a "spell," like Carl, asking both themselves and the world, "Where am I?" Sadly enough, they had no answer.

We cannot possibly answer the question "Where am I?" until we have answered the prior question "Why am I?" "What is my reason for living?" One of the shortest poems I know is fashioned in the form of a question, "I why?" With some stubbornness I would change the order to "Why I?" Ask the question any way you please, "Why I?" or "I why?" but no matter how you ask it, the answer is decisive. You can never determine where you are until you have some inkling why you are. Without some goal of meaning it matters very little where you are.

When the writers of a great Christian creed grappled with the question "Why I?" they came up with an answer that has not been improved upon in modern times. They asked, "What is the chief end of man?" and they answered, "To glorify God and enjoy Him forever." That may sound like a riddle, but it is not. It is simple as ABC and much more important. Why study and work, love and forgive, build and create? "To glorify God," said the Westminster fathers.

The meaning of the phrase "To glorify God and enjoy Him forever" is suggested in the story Gene Fowler tells of the death of Wilberforce J. Whiteman. It is to be found in an entertaining autobiographical sketch called *A Solo in Tom-Toms*. Wilberforce Whiteman was on his deathbed, and his famous son Paul hurried from New York to Denver to be with him. When the grand old man saw his son, he asked, as if remembering the pranks and troubles of other years, "Now what have you done?" Then, as if concluding a lecture on music, his favorite subject, he said, "I'll tell you why Toscanini is such a great conductor. It is because his orchestra never plays for Toscanini, nor does Toscanini reach out selfishly for credit. First, Toscanini always conducts the music as if Beethoven himself were listening. And, second, Toscanini wants Beethoven to hear it done correctly."[6]

So, Toscanini conducted his orchestra to glorify Beethoven. He wanted the music done correctly so that if Beethoven were listening he would be altogether pleased. What is more, Toscanini and his audience as well would thoroughly enjoy the music of Beethoven played the way Beethoven meant it to be played. In truth, the chief end of Toscanini's life as a musician was to glorify Beethoven and enjoy him forever. His greatness came because he never sought credit for himself, but rather lived and conducted for the glory of the great composers he honored.

The parable is altogether apt for life. The chief end of man is to play on the scales of life as if God were listening. It is to play life correctly and gloriously for the sake of the Author. Great living comes from wanting to glorify the giver of "every good and perfect gift" within us. What is more, we "enjoy" God when we glorify Him by playing life as He meant it to be played, in obedience to the mind of Christ.

In reading the gospels one is impressed by the fact that Jesus conducted his life as if the Father were listening. Those who watched him and heard him speak were convinced that "God was in Christ," and they were right. He played life correctly and gloriously as God wanted it played. Even in the crisis when the clouds were dark over Calvary, he went on playing as if he wanted God to hear the climactic notes to perfection. Said he, "If it be possible, let this cup pass from me; nevertheless, not as I will, but as thou wilt."[7] In him God was glorified, and, what is more, we see God's glory in him.

Clearly, life has glowing meaning when we live "to glorify

God." We do not live in a meaningless charade, but rather in a pattern of significance. We are linked to the great creative process wherein God is making music in our world. As Matthew Arnold put the truth,

'Tis God himself becomes apparent, when
God's wisdom and God's goodness are displayed.

So, when we live with wisdom and with goodness, we bring the life of God to the life of the world, and God is glorified in us.

That suggests another facet of meaning for life that becomes apparent when we are living "to glorify God." It is the satisfying sense of being linked to the creative will of God moving toward fulfillment in personal life and in history. A G.I. in Korea sensed the significance of life related to something beyond itself when he and Norman Cousins were riding in a jeep, bouncing over a rutted road somewhere behind the battle front. Mr. Cousins asked, "How is the morale of the men over here?" "Well," the G.I. answered, "morale is not just a matter of U.S.O. shows and free beer. To have morale you have to be connected up with the folks back home and connected up with something that really matters. The trouble here is that we just aren't connected up."[8]

Morale depends on a sense of meaning that comes from being connected up with something vital. The morale of the scientist, relentlessly pursuing the unknown, is sustained by the fact that he is connected up with the eternal truth that needs him to find it. In his pursuit of truth he is doing the will of God and glorifying God by unfolding the secrets of God's creation. The morale of the artist is sustained by the knowledge that he is connected up with the intrinsic beauty of the earth. The morale of the saint is maintained by his faith that he is connected up with the everlasting goodness of God. Life is related to, connected with, something of permanent and enduring value. It is linked to an ongoing creative process, moving in obedience to the will of God.

Charles A. Beard, the historian, expressed the conviction in simple and yet eloquent terms when he noted that there seems to be "evidence of law and plan" in the "grand drama of history." Even though disasters now and then overwhelm us and we fall into the mire, nevertheless "something magnificent is going on here." Then, with profound insight into the meaning of life and history, he noted that "the challenge to human intelligence" and spirit is "to make the finest and best in our heritage prevail." In short, life has profound meaning when we know we are connected up with "something magnificent" that is going on in the world.

Quite possibly Paul had somewhat the same notion when he noted that "the whole world has been groaning in travail together until now."[9] But the disasters and troubles that beset us and occasion the groaning are by no means in vain. The world is waiting "for our adoption as sons" and for "the redemption of our bodies."[10] So, history is the vehicle for the creation of character, the stage on which we were meant to fulfill the possibilities of ourselves and society. We are connected up with an immortal drama, linked to the eternal struggle for the Kingdom of God in ourselves and in our world. "Something magnificent" is going on here, and we may have a part in shaping its destiny in our time.

Isn't that what Jesus said with his life? On the cross he seemed to be saying that something glorious is afoot, and even a cross is not too much to pay for its fulfillment. There is a kingdom to be won through "peril, toil and pain," and you and I can have a part in shaping its destiny. We are "connected up" to the purposes of God, servants of His will, born to glorify Him in our devotion to the highest we know.

When we are connected up with the high purposes of God,

intent on glorifying Him, there is both romance and meaning in the endless task of making the most of ourselves and in discovering the unrealized powers within us. Dr. E. N. Wieman used to insist that God is "the realm of unrealized possibility" and that we experience God when we enter into that realm. We glorify God when we break through the barrier to the unattained and realize it in our own lives.

Life is full of resources and powers we have not yet discovered. The author of the little book of I Peter pointed to the fact that life is a gift with endless possibilities in it. He said, "Each has received a gift,"[11] and so it is. A baby in a crib is a bundle of possibilities. He is like a Christmas box from home with neatly wrapped packages inside waiting to be opened on the appointed day. You have to tear the wrappings off the outside to see what is inside. There are surprises for you, some things you rather expected and some things you never guessed would be there. Similarly, in yourself there are gifts you know are yours and others you have not unwrapped. There are gifts of mind to be unwrapped by discipline and gifts of courage waiting for a challenge. There are talents unsurmised that ought to be unwrapped and faith, still tied up in pretty ribbons, its power undisclosed.

"Each has received a gift"—that much is obvious. You glorify the giver when you use the gift; you dishonor the giver when you spurn the gift and leave it unused. Through all the years of my married life my wife has given me only one gift I could not use. She has bought my neckties with consummate taste with one exception. Several years ago she gave me a bright yellow and brown tie I could not wear. I wore it once at a picnic and felt conspicuous. I finally smuggled it into the summer baggage and got it to Colorado. It is still there, mercifully hidden away. But I cannot forget that necktie. It has become a family conversation piece. It represents a spurned gift, an unused gift, perversely discrediting the giver.

You cannot possibly spurn a gift with impunity, certainly not a gift of God. When you waste the good and perfect gifts of God you miss the very end of living for you cease to honor the giver. Deeper yet, you miss the inner satisfaction of fulfillment, the joy of knowing you are moving toward the goal of your high calling.

The director of public relations of a major industrial concern remarked at a dinner recently that the primary task of industry today is to give the workers some way to develop their powers of mind and hand. "As it is now," he said, "they are working in a vacuum." They push a button and they stand around most of the day watching machines make things better and faster than they ever could by hand. They think of themselves as cogs in a feelingless, meaningless machine, and there is no challenge in their toil. They have no pride in fine workmanship, no experience of growing in capacity, no sense of their own significance. In short, their gifts of hand and heart and mind are being wasted and they feel like "hollow men, headpiece filled with straw." Inevitably they are restless, unsatisfied, unhappy in their jobs, always wondering "Why I?" and finding no good reason.

It may well be that we find little in our jobs to challenge the powers and the talents hidden beneath our surface and seeming. However, the "Suggestion Box" which is becoming a part of most factories suggests that workers anywhere can be inspired to think, to use their talents of mind. What is more, the creative suggestions that often come from the workers indicate an eagerness in men to use their minds and an unconscious wish to get connected up to the creative processes of the universe itself. As an industrial engineer observed, "A worker gets greater satisfaction from seeing his suggestion adopted than from an increase in pay."

Life finds its true meaning when we are growing in knowledge and wisdom, courage and faith, with the gifts of God flowering in us. The tragedy of life is not that our talents may be meager but that we have failed to use what gifts we have. Thomas Wolfe pictured the essence of meaninglessness in his description of a collection of nondescript men in front of a cigar store waiting. Waiting for what? Waiting for nothing, nothing at all. But there are millions of men and women in homes and in businesses, in factories and in government offices who are just waiting for nothing, with no thought of seeking out their undiscovered powers and talents and gifts. Their lives are haunted by boredom. They are without the inspiration of high meaning.

But God's Kingdom awaits the revealing of the sons of God, the flowering of talents and powers, wisdom and love. It awaits men and women who will glorify God by the high use of the gifts within them. Now and then a man like Albert Schweitzer emerges to suggest our human possibilities. Theologian, philosopher, physician, great organist, and inspiring missionary, Schweitzer has fulfilled his possibilities in an amazing way. Everything he has touched has challenged his powers and stirred him to unwrap the gifts of God. In a unique way he has glorified God by the high use of his talents.

While it is perfectly true that Schweitzer is a gifted man, it also is true that many men and women possess native gifts equal to those of Dr. Schweitzer. Most of us, however, are quite unwilling to pay the price in terms of discipline and devotion that Dr. Schweitzer has paid. We are not driven as he has been driven by a resolute will to glorify God. But neither do we find the meaning he has found in life. He owns almost nothing but the clothes he wears, but there are few men who know the satisfaction and the peace he has found. His life is shot through with a sense of meaning, of connectedness to the will and purposes of God, and the gifts of his mind and heart have flowered.

Dr. Schweitzer leads us to still another facet of meaning for our lives. The missionary doctor ministering to the backward peoples of Africa is a symbol of the gifted life dedicated to the service of others. He knows his gifts are not merely his own. They were meant to be useful to the commonwealth of men under God.

There were wise men of old who received the gift of prophecy, but the prophet's gifts were not his own. He was "one man who made the many see." To be sure, the gifts in us we nourish and bring to flower are a boon to us, but they were meant to build the Kingdom here. My gifts of mind are mine to share and not to keep, and so are yours. "You are the light of the world,"[12] but lights hidden under a bushel cannot guide the feet of other men.

The gifts and powers we possess are ours as a contribution to the common life of men. Charles Kettering wisely remarked of Thomas Edison, "As truly as though each one of us had been named in his last will and testament, every one of us is a beneficiary of the labors of this man." Edison toiled far beyond the call of duty, in season and out of season, for our common wealth. As he came to the close of his amazing career, he found sublime meaning for his life in what his labors meant to other men.

It is in our ministry to other men and women that we find another basic answer to the question "Why I?" Shared gifts enrich and bless our days, but unshared gifts will leave us wondering: "Where am I?" Once I listened with delight to the stories of three businessmen who had been retired at sixty-five. One of them, nicknamed Mr. Zero by the office help, was having a bad time with himself. He had been coldly efficient in business, without the warmth of friendship, resolutely determined to provide for himself in old age. But life is altogether empty now, and time is heavy on his hands. He still is Mr. Zero, a lonely, pathetic figure, just waiting to die and wondering "Why I?"

The second man, whose gifts as a business executive were great, had used his gifts of mind and spirit to enrich the lives of others. Generous and warmhearted, he left an encouraging word wherever he went. He shared his faith and was forever doing thoughtful things. He went to Florida when he retired, but not to go to seed. He found he had a knack for fixing things, and so, with cheerful good will, he became the neighborhood handyman. He can repair anything, from a dripping faucet to a lawn mower, and he is having a wonderful time as Mr. Fixit. He takes no money for his work. He does not need it, but he is winning a wealth of satisfaction giving himself away, using his newly found gift to minister helpfully to other men.

The third man, also a business executive, went to California when he retired. At sixty-five he discovered he had a green thumb, a genius with growing things. He loves peonies and roses and he shares them with a whole neighborhood. He is having the time of his life bearing bouquets hither and yon, leaving a touch of God's beauty here and there. Life is just beginning for him. He does not need to ask, "Why I?" He knows, and life is full to overflowing.

The meaning of your life is measured in the end by what your life has meant to other men. Long ago a gracious friend proposed a motto good for any man: "Leave the trail better than you find it." It was a camper's motto, but it will do as well for life. Your gifts were meant to leave people better than you found them, wiser, nobler, more hopeful than they were before you passed their way. That is what Peter meant when he wrote, "Minister to one another."[13] He did not mean you were to go about prying into the business of other people, meddling in their affairs without an invitation. No, he was thinking of the impact one life ought to have on other lives.

There is an influence that flows from one life to another, an influence for good or ill. Not long ago I heard a woman say sadly of another woman: "After I see her, I always feel depressed." That woman's gifts of mind and courage, faith and hope had never come to flower. She is a sad and silent zero minus one. But there are those who lift us by their gifts of faith and stir us by their gifts of mind. It was Samuel Johnson who said of Edmund Burke, "That fellow calls forth all my powers." David Dun describes a man who sat on an important board of directors. When he died the president said of him: "Whenever we needed to make a decision demanding courage, Walter always faced the issue squarely and insisted we make the right decision. He gave courage to us all."

So we minister to one another through the impact of our influence. Our gifts may seem small, and yet the power of honest minds, courageous spirits, and generous hearts is beyond calculation. As Paul said to Timothy, "Stir up the gift that is in thee," and let it shine as a light to guide the feet of other men. The meaning of your life is measured in the end by what your gifts have meant to other men.

That brings us to the observation that what our lives mean to others and to ourselves as well depends upon our relation to Jesus Christ as Lord. He is the final touchstone of meaning for our lives, and in our loyalty and devotion to him we glorify God and get connected up to the high purposes of God for ourselves and our world. In a unique way the Master invades both life and history to measure the meaning of behavior and events. What we call progress is no more than meaningless motion unless it is movement toward the mind of Christ. Every step we take along the road from birth to death has somewhere its relation to the living Christ. Every event in history stands in judgment before his mind and spirit. Events are fraught with good or evil as they relate to him. Over and over again God confronts us with the imperative, "This is my beloved son, with whom I am well pleased; listen to him."[14] We glorify God as we hear the Master and follow him.

We shatter our sense of connectedness and lose sight of the meaning of our lives when we retreat from the high demands of his spirit. If we turn back, either in cynicism or in complacency, life loses its sense of high destiny. There is a symbol, I think, in the Pilgrims who stayed behind when the *Mayflower* set out for the New World. Nobody could blame them much for staying behind. They made two false starts in their two little ships and each time returned to port because the *Speedwell* leaked. Stephen Vincent Benét caught their mood when he wrote that "thinking it over" they decided "we'll go back to London," and when they got there

> Felt doubtless that queer blend of relief and shame
> Which comes to those who make sensible decisions.
> . . . .
> And yet one wonders
> What they thought later.[15]

No doubt there are times when it seems sensible to turn back from following the Master. At least, by turning back, we can keep on the safe side of things and look out for ourselves. We will not have to worry about the impact of our lives on other lives. We can simply use our gifts, such as they are, for ourselves. There won't be any necessity for worrying about glorifying God from day to day. And yet, when life has come to its sunset, one wonders what we will think then?

It seems strange how often we turn back. Lured by the vision of Christ, we set out bravely to follow where he leads. But he leads us where we would rather not go. He asks us to do what we would rather not do. He asks us to love when we feel like hating; to forgive when we feel like getting even. He bids us speak the truth when a lie would be much more convenient, and calls us to integrity when cheating would get us a better return on our investment. So we turn back, with a mixture of shame and relief that comes from a sensible decision. And yet, we always have to think about it later, remembering the glory we glimpsed and then let slip from our grasp.

We need to remember that the victors in life are those who push on in faith despite what seems sensible. Paul said of himself and his contemporaries, "We are fools for Christ's sake,"[16] and it was so. Like Moses and Abraham, they caught sight of life's promises and possibilities and "they were persuaded of them and embraced them."[17] They hung on grimly even when things were against them and the chance of triumph seemed slight. They were persuaded that what ought to be, could be. It seemed absurd to think that a handful of Christians could "upset the world" and fashion "the shape of things to come." Nevertheless, by faith, they did precisely that.

The fools in God's world are not those who stake their lives on ideals and dreams and find meaning for life in toiling for what ought to be as they see it through the mind of Christ. No, the fools are those who say: "You've got to be realistic and give up dreaming of what ought to be." Once, after Phillips Brooks had preached a sermon on brotherhood in Christ when hates were high, he received a letter bearing a single word: "Fool." The following Sunday he noted that he had received many anonymous letters to which his correspondents neglected to attach their names. "But," said he, "this is the first time I ever received a letter to which a man signed his name and forgot to write the letter."

The world said they were fools when a company of men sat down to write a constitution for thirteen states, jealous of each other, suspicious, and determined to preserve their rights. They began by saying, "We the people of these United States," when the people were not united at all. But there were those who believed that what ought to be, could be. When it looked as if the weakness of compromise would destroy all chance of unity, Washington stood up to say: "Let us raise a standard to which the wise and the just can repair. The event is in the hand of providence." It was plain to some, at least, that what ought to be, could be, and they were persuaded and embraced their dream.

Of course, it is important to notice that what ought to be is what God wants, and we glorify Him when we embrace it. We are here as pioneers and explorers, to push out the horizons of the possible, to use our gifts in the high service of what ought to be. The possibilities of our lives and of the world are like high peaks to be scaled, and Jesus Christ is at the summit, his name above every name. What is more, there is something restless in us that remains forever unsatisfied except when we are climbing toward something beyond us.

There is a symbol, I think, in the repeated efforts to scale Mount Everest, a feat finally accomplished. But why have men sought for a hundred years to conquer Everest? Why? As one explorer noted, "I suppose we want to climb Mount Everest just because it is there." That is as good an answer as any. It is the annoying challenge of the impossible that ought to be possible that lures explorers. Anyway, for a hundred years men tried unsuccessfully to scale the world's highest mountain, 29,-006 feet high, before success crowned their efforts.

Back in 1928 Mallory and Irving, famous explorers, lost their lives somewhere near the summit of Everest. When they failed to come back, their four companions who were waiting for them at the last station below the peak drew lots. Two of them set out to find their lost comrades. The other two were to wait at the base camp. The two who pushed off for the peak agreed that if they did not find the lost men they would spread their blankets on the snow in the form of a cross before they started down. Hours passed, and at last the two who watched from below saw a sign on the snow. Through the glasses they saw the sign of the cross against the heights far above.

Life is like that, and the Master calls us upward to the glorious heights of what ought to be. His name is above every name on earth, and he calls us to be pioneers. Sometimes we die still climbing and have our crosses etched against the sky. But it is better by far to go on climbing and to end on a cross than to give up and quit. It is the climbing that gives meaning to life and provides an answer to the question: "Why I?" We find significance in our striving in those moments when we are moving toward the mind of Christ, lured by that name "which is above every name." We glorify God and find high meaning to sustain morale when we are serving the highest as "good stewards of God's varied grace,"[18] for the crux of the matter is that our gifts and powers are not our own, but God's, entrusted to our keeping for threescore years and ten. With them, we were meant "to glorify God and enjoy Him forever." But we cannot glorify Him if we leave God's gifts in us unwrapped because no adventure lures us, and we cannot enjoy Him if we use our powers only to enrich ourselves. As the old hymn has it:

> Take Thou our minds, dear Lord, we humbly pray;
> Give us the mind of Christ each passing day;
> Teach us to know the truth that sets us free;
> Grant us in all our thoughts to honor Thee.[19]

Somehow we go off the track, getting all wrapped up in ourselves as if we were proprietors and not trustees of the gifts of God. Not long ago a friend sent me a book designed to help people get rich. It suggested all the techniques for getting rich in one way or another. It was full of pat formulas, sure-fire methods on how to use other people to make a fortune for oneself. I had a feeling as I read it that Dennis the Menace was on the prowl in a respectable fashion. It troubled me, because it seemed to make getting rich the crowning virtue, and it seemed to have little notion of what a man could give. It occurred to me that, after all, "God gave His son," and there was no profit in it.

Nevertheless, we go off on our own, forgetting that we are "stewards of God's varied grace." Sometimes I think God must be like a man in a restaurant trying to catch the eye of a waiter who always seems to be busy elsewhere. David McCord caught the significance of the picture in a delightful couplet when he wrote,

> By and by
> God caught his eye.

So God is forever trying to catch your eye to lure you beyond your littleness to greatness, beyond your selfishness to generosity, beyond frustration and fear and tension to strength and peace of mind. He is forever trying to make you unwrap your gifts and use them for the Kingdom's sake, "as stewards" of His manifold grace. When once God catches your eye you will know the answer to the relentless question: "Why I?"

Notes

CHAPTER I

[1] *Dennis the Menace,* by Hank Ketcham, Henry Holt and Company, 1952 (back cover).
[2] Genesis 3:12.
[3] *Hamlet,* by William Shakespeare, Act V, Scene 2.
[4] Mark 14:50.
[5] Mark 14:18.
[6] Romans 1:14.
[7] Matthew 18:20.
[8] *A Portrait of Jesus,* by Sherwood Eddy, Harper & Brothers, New York, 1943, p. 33.

CHAPTER II

[1] Mark 2:9.
[2] Genesis 4:13.
[3] *The Story of San Michele,* by Axel Munthe, J. Murray, London, 1929.
[4] Luke 17:21 (King James Version).
[5] *Rubáiyát,* by Omar Khayyám.
[6] *Paradise Lost,* by John Milton, Book I.
[7] John 8:7.
[8] Matthew 23:33.
[9] "Thoughts Suggested on the Banks of Nith," by William Wordsworth.
[10] James 5:16.
[11] *Paradise Lost,* by John Milton, Book II.
[12] Hymn by Frances Ridley Havergal.
[13] Romans 1:16.
[14] Hosea 11:8.

[15] Isaiah 1:5.

[16] Psalm 32:1-2 (Moffatt Translation).

CHAPTER III

[1] *Newsweek,* June 5, 1950.

[2] *The Cocktail Party,* by T. S. Eliot, Harcourt, Brace and Company, New York, 1950, p. 111. Used by permission of the publisher.

[3] *A Peculiar Treasure,* by Edna Ferber, Doubleday and Company, Inc., New York, 1939, p. 182.

[4] *God's Men,* by Pearl S. Buck, The John Day Company, New York, 1951, p. 375.

[5] *The Neurotic Personality of Our Time,* by Karen Horney, W. W. Norton and Company, New York, 1937, p. 35.

[6] Numbers 13:33.

[7] *Poems of William Cowper,* Thomas Nelson & Sons, London, p. 167.

[8] Matthew 10:39.

[9] I Corinthians 12:4.

[10] *Walt Whitman, an American,* by Henry Seidel Canby, Houghton Mifflin Company, Boston, 1943, p. 112.

[11] *Samuel Johnson,* by Joseph Wood Krutch, Henry Holt and Company, New York, 1944, p. 267.

[12] *Mink on Weekdays,* by Felicia Lamport, Houghton Mifflin Company, Boston, 1950.

[13] *The Lure of Superiority,* by Wayland F. Vaughan, Henry Holt and Company, New York, 1928, p. 268-269.

[14] John 18:36.

[15] Numbers 14:11.

[16] John 3:16.

CHAPTER IV

[1] Quoted from *American Chronicle,* by Ray Stannard Baker, Charles Scribner's Sons, New York, 1945, p. 181.

[2] *R. E. Lee,* by Douglas Southall Freeman, Charles Scribner's Sons, New York, 1934, Vol. II, p. 395.

[3] *So Big,* by Edna Ferber, Doubleday, Doran and Company, Inc., New York, 1924.

[4] Denver *Post,* July 20, 1950.

[5] *Ibid.*

⁶ Romans 12:3.

⁷ *George Washington Carver,* by Rackham Holt, Doubleday and Company, Inc., New York, 1945, p. 146.

⁸ I Kings, 19:13.

⁹ *How to Live on Twenty-Four Hours a Day,* by Arnold Bennett, Doubleday and Company, Inc., 1910, pp. 91-92.

¹⁰ *Pioneer Preacher,* by Opal Leigh Berryman, Thomas Y. Crowell Company, New York, 1948, p. 63.

¹¹ Ephesians 3:16 (Moffatt).

¹² Isaiah 26:3.

CHAPTER V

¹ "Elegy in a Country Churchyard," by Thomas Gray.

² *The Task,* by William Cowper, Thomas Nelson & Sons, London.

³ *The Art of Conducting Public Worship,* by Albert W. Palmer, The Macmillan Company, New York, 1939, p. 91. Used by permission of the publisher.

⁴ Psalm 23:3.

⁵ Luke 4:14.

⁶ Luke 9:29.

⁷ Psalm 46:10.

⁸ Philippians 4:7.

⁹ Philippians 4:13 (Moffatt).

¹⁰ Psalm 23:4.

¹¹ John 1:5.

¹² Isaiah 55:1-2.

¹³ Psalm 23:3.

¹⁴ "What Makes a Good Novel," by Somerset Maugham, New York *Times* Book Review, November 30, 1947.

¹⁵ "Why Men Climb Toward the Skies," by James Ramsey Ullman, New York *Times* Magazine, October 27, 1946.

¹⁶ Philippians 4:7.

¹⁷ Romans 1:16.

CHAPTER VI

¹ *The Last Puritan,* by George Santayana, Charles Scribner's Sons, New York, 1936, p. 276.

[2] *George Washington Carver,* by Rackham Holt, Doubleday and Company, Inc., New York, 1945, p. 153.

[3] *Animal Farm,* by George Orwell, Harcourt, Brace and Company, New York, 1946, pp. 4-5.

[4] *A Way of Life,* by William Osler, Remington-Putnam Book Company, Baltimore, 1932, p. 25.

[5] *Mrs. Miniver,* by Jan Struther, Harcourt, Brace and Company, New York, 1940, pp. 220-221.

[6] Isaiah 40:9.

[7] Psalm 121:1.

[8] Psalm 121:2.

[9] *Mrs. Miniver,* p. 221.

[10] Psalm 46:10.

[11] Isaiah 26:3.

[12] Proverbs 3:6.

[13] *The Screwtape Letters,* by C. S. Lewis, The Macmillan Company, New York, 1944.

[14] *American Chronicle,* by Ray Stannard Baker, Charles Scribner's Sons, New York, 1945, p. 244.

[15] *Country Editor,* by Henry Beetle Hough, Doubleday Doran and Company, Inc., New York, 1940.

CHAPTER VII

[1] "The Charge of the Light Brigade," by Alfred, Lord Tennyson.

[2] Psalm 37:5.

[3] I Peter 5:8.

[4] I Peter 4:12.

[5] Luke 13:32-33.

[6] Acts 4:20.

[7] Matthew 7:24-27.

[8] II Corinthians 4:8-9.

[9] II Corinthians 4:11.

[10] I Corinthians 13:8.

[11] Hebrews 12:27.

[12] I Peter 4:8.

[13] *The Firstborn,* by Christopher Fry, Oxford University Press, Inc., London, 1952, p. 32. Used by permission of the publisher.

[14] I Corinthians 13:8.

[15] *The Talley Method,* a play in three acts, by S. N. Behrman, Random House, New York, 1941, p. 194.

[16] Anonymous.

[17] I Peter 1:13.

[18] I Peter 5:7.

[19] *Lost in the Stars,* by Maxwell Anderson, dramatization of *Cry, the Beloved Country,* by Alan Paton, William Sloane Associates, Inc., New York, p. 51. Copyright, 1949, by Maxwell Anderson and Kurt Weill; 1950, by Maxwell Anderson. Used by permission of the publisher.

CHAPTER VIII

[1] *Psychology and Religion for Everyday Living,* by Charles T. Holman, The Macmillan Company, New York, 1949, p. 81.

[2] *Humanity and Happiness,* by Georg Bochman, The Viking Press, New York, 1950, p. 72.

[3] *The Scarlet Fish and Other Stories,* Methuen, London.

[4] "Battle Cry," from *Collected Poems,* by John G. Neihardt, The Macmillan Company, New York, 1926, p. 133.

[5] From: "If" from *The Five Nations,* by Rudyard Kipling. Copyright, 1910, by Rudyard Kipling, reprinted by permission of Mrs. George Bambridge, Doubleday & Company, Inc., and A. P. Watt & Son.

[6] II Corinthians 12:9.

[7] Philippians 4:13.

[8] I John 4:18.

[9] Romans 8:31.

[10] Isaiah 30:15.

[11] *Beauchamp's Career,* by George Meredith, Charles Scribner's Sons, New York, rev. ed., 1897.

[12] II Corinthians 4:18.

[13] Luke 22:42.

[14] *Macbeth,* by William Shakespeare, Act V.

[15] II Corinthians 4:16-18.

CHAPTER IX

[1] "Sonnet, on Seeing the Elgin Marbles," by John Keats.

[2] *Queen Victoria,* by E. F. Benson, Grosset and Dunlap, 1935, p. 206.

[3] *Beethoven,* by Robert H. Schauffler, Doubleday and Company, Inc., New York, 1929, p. 378.

[4] Psalm 91:6.

[5] *Nathaniel Hawthorne, the American Years,* by Robert Cantwell, Rinehart and Company, Inc., New York, 1948, p. 343.

[6] *The Happy Man,* by Robert Easton, The Viking Press, New York, 1943, p. 11.

[7] Quoted from *The Art of Living Today,* by Douglas Horton, Sermon Collection published by the United Church of Hyde Park, Chicago, 1935, p. 32-33.

[8] Matthew 6:28.

[9] "We See As We Are," by William Channing Gannett, from *The Thought of God in Hymns and Poems,* The Beacon Press, Boston, 1894, p. 114.

[10] *A Testament of Devotion,* by Thomas Kelly, Harper & Brothers, New York, 1941, p. 57.

[11] *Each in His Own Tongue,* by William Herbert Carruth.

[12] Exodus 3:5.

CHAPTER X

[1] *The Life of Andrew Jackson,* by Marquis James, Garden City Publishing Company, Garden City, New York, 1940, p. 640.

[2] *Abraham Lincoln,* by Carl Sandburg, Charles Scribner's Sons, New York, 1943, Vol. II, p. 168.

[3] Luke 24:28.

[4] *Poems of William Cowper* ("Conversation"), Thomas Nelson & Sons, London, p. 276.

[5] Luke 4:8.

[6] James 1:6 (King James Version).

[7] Matthew 22:37.

[8] *University Debater's Manual,* The H. W. Wilson Co., New York, 1931, p. 145.

[9] *The Firstborn,* by Christopher Fry, Oxford University Press, Inc., London, 1952, p. 14. Used by permission of the publisher.

[10] Matthew 5:38-39.

[11] Joshua 24:15.

[12] I Corinthians 13:8 (King James Version).

[13] Matthew 5:6.

[14] John 14:6.

[15] John 7:17.

CHAPTER XI

[1] "The People Will Live On," from *The People, Yes,* by Carl Sandburg, Harcourt, Brace and Company, 1936.

[2] Matthew 4:4.

[3] New York *Times,* Harry Hansen.

[4] Article by Clarence Woodbury in *The Nation's Business,* June, 1954, p. 74.

[5] "The Hollow Men," by T. S. Eliot, from *Collected Poems.* Copyright, 1936, by Harcourt, Brace and Company, New York, p. 101. Used by permission of the publisher.

[6] *A Solo in Tom-Toms,* by Gene Fowler, The Viking Press, New York, 1946, p. 242.

[7] Matthew 26:39.

[8] Evanston Peace Rally address, May 28, 1954.

[9] Romans 8:22.

[10] Romans 8:23.

[11] I Peter 4:10.

[12] Matthew 5:14.

[13] I Peter 4:10 (King James Version).

[14] Mark 9:7.

[15] *Western Star,* by Stephen Vincent Benét published by Rinehart & Company, Inc., p. 128. Copyright, 1943, by Rosemary Carr Benét. Used by permission of the publisher.

[16] I Corinthians 4:10.

[17] Hebrews 11:13 (King James Version).

[18] I Peter 4:10.

[19] Hymn by the Rev. William H. Foukes.

Index

Set in Intertype Garamond
Format by Marguerite Swanton
Manufactured by The Haddon Craftsmen, Inc.
Published by HARPER & BROTHERS, *New York*